TIMING
RESISTANCE
TRAINING

Programming the Muscle Clock
for Optimal Performance

TIMING RESISTANCE TRAINING

Programming the Muscle Clock for Optimal Performance

Amy Ashmore, PhD

HUMAN KINETICS

Library of Congress Cataloging-in-Publication Data

Names: Ashmore, Amy, 1971- author.
Title: Timing resistance training: Programming the muscle clock for optimal performance / Amy Ashmore, PhD.
Description: Champaign, Illinois : Human Kinetics, 2019. | Includes
 bibliographical references and index.
Identifiers: LCCN 2019003114 (print) | LCCN 2019006796 (ebook) | ISBN
 9781492591368 (epub) | ISBN 9781492589990 (PDF) | ISBN 9781492589990
 (print)
Subjects: LCSH: Exercise therapy. | Muscles--Physiology. | Muscle strength. |
 Periodization training. | Physical fitness--Physiological aspects.
Classification: LCC RM725 (ebook) | LCC RM725 .A845 2019 (print) | DDC
 615.8/2--dc23
LC record available at https://lccn.loc.gov/2019003114

ISBN: 978-1-4925-8999-0 (print)

Senior Acquisitions Editor: Roger W. Earle; **Senior Developmental Editor:** Cynthia McEntire; **Managing Editor:** Dominique J. Moore; **Copyeditor:** Chernow Editorial Services; **Indexer**: Beth Nauman-Montana; **Permissions Manager:** Dalene Reeder; **Graphic Designer:** Whitney Milburn; **Cover Designer:** Keri Evans; **Cover Design Associate:** Susan Rothermel Allen; **Photograph (cover):** Tarasov_vl/iStock/Getty Images; **Photographs (interior):** © Human Kinetics; **Photo Asset Manager:** Laura Fitch; **Photo Production Coordinator**: Amy M. Rose; **Photo Production Manager:** Jason Allen; **Senior Art Manager:** Kelly Hendren; **Illustrations:** © Human Kinetics; **Printer:** Versa Press

Human Kinetics books are available at special discounts for bulk purchase. Special editions or book excerpts can also be created to specification. For details, contact the Special Sales Manager at Human Kinetics.

Printed in the United States of America   10   9   8   7   6   5   4   3   2   1
The paper in this book is certified under a sustainable forestry program.

Human Kinetics
P.O. Box 5076
Champaign, IL 61825-5076
Website: www.HumanKinetics.com

In the United States, email info@hkusa.com or call 800-747-4457.
In Canada, email info@hkcanada.com.
In the United Kingdom/Europe, email hk@hkeurope.com.

For information about Human Kinetics' coverage in other areas of the world,
please visit our website: **www.HumanKinetics.com**

E7482

Tell us what you think!
Human Kinetics would love to hear what we can do to improve the customer experience. Use this QR code to take our brief survey.

For Aiden Slade

CONTENTS

PART II LEARN THE TOOLS
FOR EXERCISE PROGRAMMING

PART III CREATE EFFECTIVE
TRAINING PROGRAMS

PREFACE

If you are reading this book, it is safe to say that you have an interest in muscle strength and power development and resistance training programming. You also have knowledge of the latest research in muscle physiology, and you are excited, like I am, about the discovery of muscle clocks and what they mean to the future of resistance training and sport performance.

What muscle clocks tell us is that muscles are not simple effectors under nervous system control; they are intelligent and autonomous structures that—with the right cues from us—can learn to anticipate upcoming training sessions and improve performance. The key to understanding and working with muscle clocks is strategic timing.

Sport scientists have known since periodization training emerged in the Soviet Union in the 1950s that timing is one of the most critical programming variables influencing peak athletic performance. Although this book builds on the existing knowledge of periodization, it looks at muscles and resistance training programming in a new way. The origin of this book is a 16-week professional boxing conditioning program that was executed and documented at Las Vegas's Top Rank gym in the late 1990s. During the years I spent inside elite-level professional boxing gyms, I noticed two trends about their highly effective conditioning programs: the consistent and long-term use of similar exercises and the adherence to strict timing guidelines. Years later I aligned what boxing was doing with new research on muscle clocks and new ways to think about timing to develop a new approach to resistance training programming.

This book was written with three different groups of people in mind:

- Strength and power development practitioners and coaches
- Personal fitness trainers, athletic trainers, and physical therapists who work with athletes and elite fitness enthusiasts
- Knowledgeable athletes and fitness enthusiasts who understand the concepts and can apply the guidelines to their own workouts and programs

This book is organized into three parts: Understand the Science of Muscle Clocks, Learn the Tools for Exercise Programming, and Create Effective Training Programs.

Chapter 1 explores what muscle clocks are and what their discovery means to the future of resistance training and sport performance. The chapter describes research showing that each one of our over 600 skeletal muscles has its own inner time clock, termed a *muscle clock*, and when it is destroyed, muscle function is adversely affected, illustrating the critical role of muscle clocks to muscle performance.

Chapter 2 examines interference theory, the scientific evidence showing that when cardiovascular endurance training is done closely in time with resistance training it interferes with muscle strength and power outcomes. The chapter explores suggested mechanisms of inference and how to program resistance training and cardiovascular endurance training to avoid it.

Chapter 3 discusses the three types of timing cues that muscle clocks use to monitor training time intervals and relates those cues to common periodization programming variables. The chapter also includes a discussion on the use of nonconsecutive days off, termed *intermittent rest*, and details how it is applied to exercise programming, high-intensity interval training, and recovery.

Chapter 4 makes recommendations for specific exercises to use in later chapters to build paired exercise workouts for strength and power outcomes along with use in concurrent and flexibility training programs. Based on the timing cues exercises deliver to muscle clocks, exercises are grouped into six categories: all-body power, bilateral lower body, unilateral lower body, upper body, isolation, and plyometric. Exercises are broken down and analyzed by the primary joints used and muscle actions to establish the foundation for the biomechanically paired workout method.

Chapter 5 introduces anticipation training, a form of training that relies on the strategic use of timing to speak to muscle clocks and teach muscles to anticipate. Borrowing from motor learning concepts, this chapter examines the similarities between neural and muscle anticipation and how muscle clocks use both types of anticipation to improve resistance training outcomes. Research summary statements at the end of the chapter provide you with ways to immediately apply the concepts to resistance training programming.

Chapter 6 explores the idea of intentional undertraining. The chapter explains that undertraining is a viable training method when the timing of scheduled exercise and activity–rest phases are used as the primary variables for programming. When a resistance training program that focuses on timing is consistently performed, certain molecular actions occur within muscle and recovery becomes optimized, enhancing performance. Intentional undertraining is discussed in direct contrast to a training system that focuses on volume and intensity alone, which exhausts muscles and often leads to overtraining.

Finally, in chapters 7 through 10, I put it all together to use the paired exercise method to create new strength, power, concurrent, and flexibility training workouts and programs that speak to muscle clocks. Using earlier concepts, such as interference avoidance, muscle anticipation, intentional undertraining, intermittent rest, and complex training, I show you how to use suggested exercises along with strategic timing to build new resistance training workouts and programs.

ACKNOWLEDGMENTS

Thank you to Mitch Hampp at Top Rank Boxing for giving me a place to work in the gym and the ability to document the training programs in which I first recognized the role of timing to muscle performance. Thank you, Dexter, for the years in the gyms in Texas, Mexico, and Las Vegas.

PART I | UNDERSTAND THE SCIENCE OF MUSCLE CLOCKS

Timing is the key to resistance training success, from the origins of sport training in periodization to the many and varied training methods used today. Successful resistance training programming relies on strategic timing: what time of day and how often training is scheduled, how long an exercise session lasts, intraset (within set) breaks, and even the speed of muscle contractions. Although it is well known that timing is critical to resistance training, scientists have just begun to understand how timing is monitored and taken into account by muscles via newly discovered muscle clocks.

Chapter 1 explores what muscle clocks are and what they mean to the future of resistance training. Muscle clocks are one of many internal biological clocks, including the master clock in the brain and the many other tissue-specific clocks such as bone, tendon, and cartilage clocks, that have the body on a 24-hour, daily rhythm. Chapter 1 explains how muscle clocks use specific cues to monitor time intervals and coordinate the molecular actions associated with resistance training outcomes to anticipated workouts. The chapter details research showing each one of the more than 600 skeletal muscles has its own inner molecular time clock that helps muscles learn to anticipate upcoming training sessions and proposing that muscles are intelligent regulators that cause action rather than only respond to central nervous system commands. Combining the knowledge gained through new research on muscle inner time clocks with traditional periodization training, chapter 1 shows readers how muscle clocks increase muscle mass, strength, and power along with improved recovery.

The timing of all workouts is critical because it helps avoid interference or competition between modes of exercise. Chapter 2 examines interference theory, its mechanisms, and ways to develop resistance training workouts and programs to avoid it. Resistance training and cardiovascular exercise are competing modes of exercise that initiate different muscle molecular actions and confuse muscles. When cardiovascular and resistance training are performed within a single session or even within the same day, muscle performance can be adversely affected. This is because muscles look for consistent cues to know which molecular actions to click on. The molecular actions associated with different types of exercise outcomes are unique and seek different cues. When cues are unalike, such as jogging and a squat, and occur within an hour of each other, muscles do not know what to do, so they shut down, and performance is negatively affected.

The first part of chapter 2 discusses in detail what causes muscle confusion at a molecular level. The chapter explains the research that shows how the mode, frequency, volume, intensity, and duration of training sessions cause interference in muscles and contribute to negative training outcomes. The second part of the chapter acknowledges that the real-life dilemma is that the vast majority of athletic and fitness programs must include both resistance and cardiovascular modes of exercise; therefore, the chapter also provides readers with solutions, showing how to build workouts and programs to avoid interference.

1 | What Is a Muscle Clock?

Although science has known about the existence of the master clock since the early 1970s (24), the discovery of muscle clocks is relatively new. The existence of muscle clocks was first proposed in 1998 by Zylka and colleagues (29). Studies have shown that when muscle clocks are destroyed, skeletal muscles are adversely affected. Muscles weaken and display decreased mitochondrial content and function (1, 11). Although muscle clock function is not completely understood, and scientists are just beginning to understand the significance of muscle clocks and their effect on muscle performance, it is clear that muscle clocks act to regulate muscle function and are significant to sport performance.

The goal of all internal clocks is to align the body with the outside environment on a 24 h schedule, creating a circadian rhythm that prepares the body for daily environmental changes such as night and day and influences sleep and activity times.

Muscle Clocks: Description and Functions

Muscle clocks are transcription factors or genes inside each muscle that regulate physiological cycles according to environmental changes and physical activity. The primary function of muscle clocks is to monitor what happens outside and inside the body during a 24 h period. To help muscles function optimally, muscle clocks pay careful attention to things such as day–night phases, activity–rest cycles, hormone levels, body temperature, and eating and exercise habits.

The discovery of these internal, autonomous regulating clocks in muscle is significant because it shifts how we think about muscles. Muscles are not simply responding to central nervous system commands; instead, the muscles themselves are able to cause action.

Muscle clocks play a role in regulating muscle function. They also communicate with each other, the musculoskeletal system, the brain, and the entire body. Muscle clocks synchronize muscles to the master biological clock in the brain. They also connect muscles to other periphery clocks located in tissues inside and outside the musculoskeletal system.

Muscle clocks are like internal pacemakers. At the cellular level, a molecular clock provides an essential timekeeping method to prepare the muscle for daily changes in the environment. The capacity to synchronize the molecular clock and intracellular activity with outside events, such as day–night cycles, indicates an ability to adapt to environmental conditions. In that way, muscles are smart and show the ability to adapt to their surroundings. An example of another musculoskeletal system clock is a bone clock; an example of a periphery clock is one located in the liver.

Relationship to Muscle Tissue

Muscles make up an estimated 40% to 45% of the body's total mass. Muscle is the single most abundant tissue in the human body. It would make sense, due to its volume alone, that muscle is not simply an effector, a structure under control of the central nervous system that acts only in response to commands. Instead, muscle is an important regulator that causes action in other body systems and has capabilities beyond only responding.

Whatever muscles do affects the entire body. The finding that muscles have clocks that control their functions and communicate with other body systems is revolutionary. It shows that muscles, through a variety of cues, including strategically planned exercise, play a critical role in regulating whole body functioning. For example, with the help of muscle clocks, muscle communicates with the liver and plays an important role in maintaining metabolic homeostasis of the body.

The idea that muscles are more than effectors is not new. Because muscle mass makes up a huge percentage of the human body, it has seemed illogical to many people that muscle's only function would be to act under central nervous system command and execute movements. Although the hypothesis is not new, the evidence to support the idea is new and is explored in detail later in the chapter.

Total Quantity

There are more than 600 skeletal muscles in the human body. Each one has its own muscle clock composed of many different types of genetic material (20, 26). Because humans have more than 600 muscles and each one has its own clock, there are more than 600 individual skeletal muscle clocks working 24 h days to synchronize muscle activity to the master clock in the brain, the other musculoskeletal system clocks, the other body systems, and the environment. Muscle clocks are not one size fits all. Different muscle clocks exist in different muscles made up of different fiber types. The significance of the various types of muscle clocks is discussed later in the chapter.

Composition

Muscle clocks are located inside muscles. They are made up of *transcription factors*, a sequence-specific binding *factor* that controls the rate of *transcription* of genetic information (*transcription* is the process by which genetic information from a thread of DNA is used to produce a thread of complementary RNA) and is involved in the conversion of DNA into RNA (figure 1.1). *Once DNA is converted to RNA, the RNA is used to regulate and express genes important to muscle clock function.* Transcription factors include essential proteins that initiate and regulate gene activity inside muscle. Each internal clock is made up of numerous transcriptional factors, each with a different role in controlling the clock. Among these transcription factors, some are exclusive to the core molecular clock and some are found across different types of clocks; the muscle clocks also contain genes important for skeletal muscle–specific functions, such as the proteins myosin and troponin, and others important for metabolism and ATP synthesis.

Daily Schedule

All biological clocks are on a 24 h schedule. The 24 h cycle is reflected in daily changes of the whole body, global gene expression pattern, and metabolism. In other words, the transcription factors within the muscle and other clocks behave differently at different times of the day and in response to different stimuli.

The local activity of specific peripheral tissues such as muscles reflect the 24 h cycle of their clocks. Muscle clocks learn a schedule by paying attention to cues outside of the body such as the light–dark cycle, which is associated with the time of day relative to the position of the earth's orbit and is a universal entrainment cue to all biological clocks. (*Entrainment* refers to the matching of rhythmic biological events, such as the circadian rhythm, to changes in the outside or local tissue environment.) Time-of-day cues

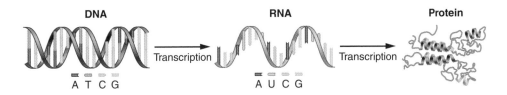

DNA   **RNA**   **Protein**

Transcription   Transcription

A T C G   A U C G

FIGURE 1.1   DNA is converted to RNA, which is used to code, decode, regulate, and express genes important to muscle clock function.

set and reset all internal clocks, including muscle clocks. The time of day is the most obvious and well understood clock cue, but as discussed in later chapters, cues are numerous and tissue specific. In the case of muscle, additional cues include hormone levels, activity–rest patterns, and exercise programming (such as the timing of resistance training), all of which are discussed at length in chapter 3.

Tissue Specificity

The clock-controlled genes that make up muscle clocks and the pathways they use to communicate are tissue specific. That means each type of peripheral clock contains its own tissue-specific genes that allow it to monitor other systems and communicate changes specific to that tissue. The internal molecular clocks in muscle cells allow them to anticipate the rhythmic daily changes in muscle and their local environment and make muscle-specific adaptations. Muscle clocks pay attention to muscles, while other peripheral clocks focus on changes occurring in other tissues (for example, bone clocks focus on bones).

The master clock resides in the brain and oversees all the clocks in the body, including the muscle clocks. The musculoskeletal system also includes cartilage, bone, and tendon clocks. As mentioned earlier, each clock is tissue specific, containing specific transcription factors to that tissue and sharing only a few. Each tissue-specific clock also behaves uniquely. When muscle, bone, and cartilage clocks are manipulated in research studies, different negative effects happen to each. For example, if the BMAL1 protein, a critical transcription factor for clock function, is knocked out in all three peripheral clocks—muscle, bone, and cartilage—different physiological events follow. In muscle, the muscle fibers become disorganized, mitochondrial dysfunction occurs, and muscle fiber size reduces (1). In addition, knocking out BMAL1 protein in muscle clocks reduces the diameter of muscle fibers and induces sarcopenia (age-dependent loss of muscle tissue) (11). Muscle regeneration also is impaired following BMAL1 protein destruction (4). These results illustrate how critical the genes that make up muscle clocks are to optimal muscle functioning and performance.

The effects of knocking out biological clocks are not isolated to muscle. When whole body BMAL1 protein, not just muscle BMAL1 protein, is knocked out, the normal activity–rest rhythm disappears in muscle and daily movement activity is reduced (11). Taken together, the muscle-specific events that occur after the BMAL1 protein genes are destroyed indicate the importance of the muscle clock in regulating muscle function and performance.

BMAL1 protein knockout creates numerous effects in muscle, but it also affects other musculoskeletal system clocks. In cartilage, a BMAL1 protein knockout negatively affects the growth plates, resulting in shorter bones (3). Also, knocking out BMAL1 protein in the bone itself results in bone loss similar to that seen with aging (19).

The takeaway message is that the same transcription factor—in this case BMAL1 protein—can cause various consequences in different tissue. The results of knocking out a transcription factor show the importance of internal regulating clocks and also highlight that there are different types of clocks found in various tissues that all have tissue-specific regulating functions. The reality of muscle tissue–specific consequences in response to losing an internal clock gene, such as the local BMAL1 protein, further illustrates the autonomy of skeletal muscles.

The focus of this book is on muscle clocks, so tendon, bone, and cartilage clocks are not fully discussed. However, it is essential to recognize that these clocks exist and that they communicate with muscle clocks to aid in optimal musculoskeletal system development and performance. They also play a role in regulating the metabolic functioning of the musculoskeletal system, helping prevent metabolic and bone disorders.

Timing Cues

Muscle clocks monitor time intervals by paying careful attention to cues, or *zeitgebers* (German for "cue," used frequently in the literature on biological clocks). Muscle clocks compare what is going on in the environment to what is happening in muscle. Time cues tell muscles what time it is and what is going on at that time both inside and outside the body so muscles can coordinate muscle molecular events. During any 24 h period, muscles are hard at work coordinating muscle activity with their environment.

The most important time cue all internal clocks receive is light. Light provides information about the time of day and activity–rest patterns. However, there are many other cues, such as hormone levels, body temperature, exercise, and eating habits, that also influence molecular clock activity; these will be discussed in detail in chapter 3. For now, what is important is to recognize that muscle clocks use cues to monitor time intervals and learn from those cues what to expect when and how to respond.

Biological Rhythms

Skeletal muscles have their own biological rhythms in search of timing-related cues. The first indication of the existence of biological rhythms in skeletal muscle came in 1986 when researchers noticed daily variations in muscle protein synthesis in rats (17). Initial observations of rhythms were not recognized as muscle clocks, and the presence of an independent circadian clock oscillator in muscle was not proposed until 1998 when Zylka and colleagues recognized it (29). In 2007, Takahashi and colleagues (25) mapped the first skeletal muscle clock, finding 215 genes in mouse and 107 in rat skeletal muscle, each with unique rhythmic patterns of expression related to timing cues. Other researchers in 2007 were able to identify more than 200 rhythmic genes in rat skeletal muscle (13, 14).

The research on muscle clocks has advanced rapidly, and scientists now know that rhythmic genes depend on muscle fiber type (8). In addition to muscle fiber specificity, many more rhythmic genes have been discovered. In animal studies, 684 rhythmic genes were identified in the fast-twitch tibialis anterior muscle, but 1,359 rhythmic genes were identified in the slow-twitch soleus muscle (8).

Due to the discovery of these rhythmic genes in muscles, researchers can safely deduce that the musculoskeletal system plays a role in setting and resetting the whole body's daily rest–activity phases. The specific roles of various tissues have not yet been determined, and the extent to which skeletal muscle is autonomous and the influence of scheduled exercise on rhythms and functions are still being studied.

Muscles do not work alone. When influencing whole body system rhythms, muscles work in conjunction with connective tissue, bone, and cartilage; thus what affects those tissues can in turn affect muscle and the whole body circadian rhythm. Specific catabolic (which cause tissue breakdown) and anabolic (which build tissue) timing mechanisms have been identified in mouse cartilage, where the majority of catabolic genes peak early in the day, following the nighttime phase of mice (11). However, the anabolic genes peak 12 h later, early at night. A similar peak time of anabolic genes was observed in muscle, indicating muscle tissue in mice is most likely to grow 12 h after the night phase. The timing of rhythmic catabolic and anabolic activity of musculoskeletal system tissues is important because it shows synchronization. The catabolic–anabolic rhythms in mouse and rat cartilage and muscle are similar to what is widely accepted in humans (11). (This is addressed in detail in part III.) The bottom line is that the mapped biological cycle of catabolism and anabolism in rodents coincides with data that support the time of day of anticipated human muscle growth potential.

One more important note regards cartilage cycles and how they affect muscle performance. Dudek and Meng (7) suggest that chronic decoupling of the musculoskeletal metabolic cycles and the animal's daily activity could lead to degenerative changes in cartilage and overall reduced performance in muscles. On the other hand, synchrony among different musculoskeletal tissues could play a critical role in positive muscle physiology. In support of the effect different musculoskeletal system tissues have on one another, the loss of circadian rhythm in cartilage results in shorter bones in mice (7). It can be expected that if one aspect of the musculoskeletal system is out of phase, other systems, such as muscles, will also be affected.

Muscle clocks use exercise training and programming cues to help regulate muscle performance and coordinate the musculoskeletal system and other internal body systems. Resistance training provides the cues muscles look for, such as mode (type of exercise and biomechanics), frequency, duration, volume, intensity, and rest periods, all of which are discussed in detail in chapter 3.

The Master Clock

Biological clocks are organized into a hierarchal structure. The master clock in the brain (figure 1.2) communicates with all of the clocks in the periphery. Scientists have known about the master clock's existence since the 1970s, and the fact that it is responsible for circadian or biological rhythms has been known for quite a long time. The master clock explains why long-haul flights disrupt sleep patterns and why shift workers are prone to ill health when not on a regular schedule. (Or in some cases, a night shift only schedule affects healthy circadian functioning.) Biological clocks crave consistency, and they look for the cues to create it, including exercise training and programming cues.

When the master clock is knocked out, circadian rhythms are interrupted (12). The master clock imposes rhythmicity to peripheral organs such as skeletal muscle, tendons, cartilage, and bone. For a long time, until the discovery of peripheral clocks, it was thought that the central clock was the only internal pacemaker, independently governing the circadian rhythm in all tissues, including all of the musculoskeletal system clocks.

Whereas the master clock exerts influence over all of the peripheral clocks, the peripheral clocks have no pacemaking effect on the master clock. This is a very important concept. The peripheral clocks, including muscle clocks, do not influence the master clock. The master clock reigns supreme and has influence over all peripheral clocks. However, peripheral clocks do contain features such as their own circadian rhythms and entrainment methods, which provide them some autonomy from the master clock. For muscle clocks, entrainment cues, such as the timing of exercise and specific exercise training and programming features, give muscles autonomy.

The bottom line is that local clocks, such as muscle clocks, prepare local tissues for specific demands associated with environmental and internal changes but do not affect the master clock. However, as discussed later in the chapter, repeated skeletal muscle contraction can influence the master clock.

Suprachiasmatic Nucleus

The master clock is located in the suprachiasmatic nucleus (SCN) of the hypothalamus, located deep in the anterior (front) part of the brain (figure 1.2). The SCN is a cluster of neurons that recognize night–day cycles and keep the body on the 24 h cycle that is important to muscle and all other peripheral clocks. The SCN can keep the rest of the body on an approximately 24 h schedule even in the absence of light.

Destroying sections of the SCN do not abolish the peripheral clocks, including muscle clocks (5). However, destruction of the SCN can lead to desynchronization of internal peripheral clocks and other regulating body systems. The fact that destroying the SCN does not destroy the ability of

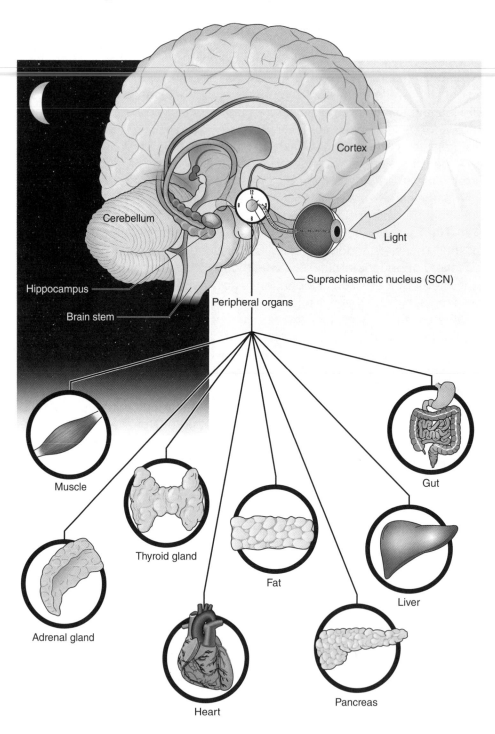

FIGURE 1.2   The master clock located in the suprachiasmatic nucleus in the brain influences the many peripheral biological clocks throughout the body, primarily relaying information about time of day and light–dark cycles. Internal clocks do not directly influence the master clock.

muscle clocks to stay on a 24 h schedule is important because it supports the notion that muscle clocks and muscles are autonomous.

Direct Influence of the Master Clock on Muscle Clocks

The master clock in the brain influences all peripheral clocks, including muscle, tendon, bone, and cartilage clocks, and many more throughout the body. Because the master clock recognizes light cycles, it helps keep muscle clocks on 24 h schedules, but the master clock is not the only regulator. Each tissue has its own clock that responds to tissue-specific cues, such as the timing and type of exercise in muscles. Specific cues, along with information from the master clock and environment, help clocks differentiate times of day and set a schedule.

Lack of Influence by Muscle Clocks

Muscle clocks do not influence the master clock directly. Although the master clock is essential to peripheral clock functioning, the peripheral clocks do not exert a direct influence on the master clock. Whereas the master clock sends signals to the peripheral clocks about the time of day and activity–rest cycles, the peripheral clocks do not relay information back to the master clock.

Although muscle clocks do not directly influence the master clock, skeletal muscles can influence the master clock indirectly via repeated muscle contraction. The master clock, like muscle clocks, is influenced by exercise. In other words, muscle clocks might not directly affect the master clock, but the action of muscles can, suggesting again that muscles are autonomous regulators instead of only effectors.

In terms of how muscle action influences the master clock, the master clock responds to the timing of exercise as well as multiple bouts of scheduled exercise. When the effects of exercise on the master clock were examined, it was found that scheduled exercise is recognized by the master clock as an entrainment cue (20, 21). Exercise functions to aid the SCN in adapting to the environment, providing cues about activity–rest cycles. The changes in local gene expression associated with the daily loading and unloading of muscle caused by exercise and its related metabolic changes are an important part of the whole body circadian rhythm. The master clock and light–day cycle can be overridden by regularly scheduled exercise, indicating that peripheral tissues, such as muscle, have flexibility in how they respond to the environment and other time cues (6, 18, 25).

Regularly scheduled exercise affords muscles autonomy and flexibility in responding to the demands of their unique environment. Exercise studies in mice suggest there is an optimal time of day for exercise to enhance the circadian rhythms. However, in terms of optimizing the role of muscle clocks in muscle performance, an ideal time for humans to exercise has not yet been determined; therefore, until more is known about a suggested time of day to train, consistently timed daily exercise is the viable alternative (26).

Regulation and Communication

Muscle clocks provide stability, help set schedules, and teach muscles when to turn on molecular actions in anticipation of daily environmental and activity changes. To communicate with one another and other body systems, skeletal muscles use a specific signaling pathway to send messages.

Effect of Myokine Release

Muscle action is communicated internally and to the rest of the body using myokines, proteins specific to muscle. When a muscle contracts, it releases myokines, the chemical messengers that muscles and other tissues understand as a reflection of muscle activity (figure 1.3). The myokines relay timing cues about when a muscle is active relative to the time of day. Repeated, scheduled muscle contractions relay cues such as activity–rest cycles and timing of exercise.

Myokines can be thought of as chemical messengers telling the rest of the body what is going on in muscles and when. They are released into tissue circulation and are responsible for relaying the timing of exercise as an entrainment cue to muscles, the musculoskeletal system, master clock, and whole body (16). Myokines synchronize muscles to other systems, which improves musculoskeletal system performance and aligns functions such as sleep and recovery to activity–rest cycles essential to performance.

Role of the Sympathetic Nervous System

The sympathetic nervous system is the biological pathway internal clocks use to relay messages. The master clock of the brain regulates neural and endocrine (hormone regulation) system functions through the use of the sympathetic nervous system (SNS). The SNS is how the master clock sends messages from the brain to the peripheral clocks about the 24 h cycle and light–dark changes. It is the pathway used to set and reset clocks on a daily schedule.

The master clock acts as a timekeeper for the whole body. Once the messages are sent from the master clock to the peripheral clocks, additional mechanisms come into play. Just as the master clock uses the SNS to relay information throughout the body, myokines also travel from muscles throughout the body via the SNS. Specifically, myokines use the autonomic nervous system (ANS) division of the SNS. The ANS receives information about the body and environment and responds with a body action. The fact that the ANS responds with action to information received from the myokines sent by the muscles is a key point. What it means is critical to the premise of muscle autonomy—muscles are not only effectors but are able to use myokines to communicate, influence, and cause action throughout the entire body.

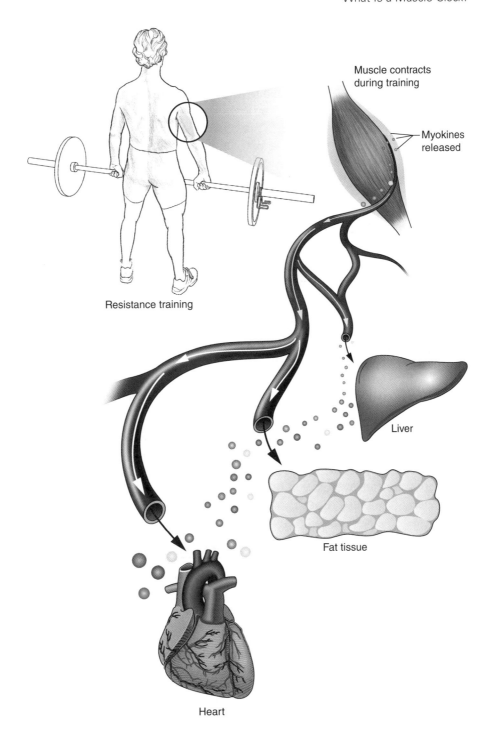

Resistance training

Muscle contracts during training

Myokines released

Liver

Fat tissue

Heart

FIGURE 1.3 Myokines are released during resistance training. Resistance training causes muscle fibers to contract. This stimulates the release of myokines that crosstalk and network with other structures in the musculoskeletal system and throughout the body. Myokines relay cues about the timing of resistance training, allowing muscles and other structures to anticipate upcoming workout sessions and improve muscle performance.

Muscle–Organ Crosstalk

The idea that skeletal muscle influences other tissues is no longer novel. It is clear that muscles network with one another and other tissues and systems; this interaction is commonly called *crosstalk*. It is also evident that skeletal muscle actions lead to changes in the body that aid muscle performance and recovery. Muscles communicate with organs via myokines. When a muscle contracts, myokines are released and travel to other tissues, relaying information about the timing of muscle activity. Crosstalk facilitates synchrony with other tissues to maintain matching circadian cycles. If skeletal muscle rhythms are disrupted or asynchronous, it affects the entire body.

The fact that crosstalk occurs and that information is relayed to other body systems when muscles contract is a point that is critical to the premise of this book. It highlights the value of scheduled exercise, the autonomy of muscle, and the effects of muscle as a regulator. The research on what types of exercise and how exercise entrains internal clocks is emergent, but just the idea and implications that strategic exercise programming, specifically resistance training, can set and reset internal clocks is exciting to scientists and practitioners.

Synchronization to Other Systems

Muscle clocks synchronize muscles with other body systems. Because muscle is such a large contributor to system and whole body physiology, the ability of muscles to synchronize to other systems has broad implications for human health and sport performance. The ability of skeletal muscle clocks to influence other systems suggests the power of scheduled exercise for overall health and sport performance.

Application to Resistance Training

It is clear that muscle clocks play a role in whole body circadian rhythms. However, the connection needs to be made between muscle clock entrainment and resistance training. Although the data are less numerous on the effects of resistance training on muscle clock function versus the effects of cardiovascular exercise on muscle clocks, it does exist.

Some of the first evidence of the existence of a resistance training effect on human skeletal muscle clocks showed that one bout of resistance training is associated with changes in molecular clock gene expression in the quadriceps muscle (27). The data show that 10 sets of 8 repetitions of unilateral knee extension at 80% 1RM, with 3 min rest periods between sets, were sufficient to change the core gene clock expressions. Muscles of the exercised leg were analyzed 6 and 18 h after an acute bout of resistance training and showed that genes were affected. When the unexercised leg was examined, notable changes in muscle clock gene expression were not seen. The results indicated that resistance training, specifically contractile activity, affected clock gene expression, indicating that there is an interaction between muscle contraction and the expression of clock genes in human muscle and demonstrating the role of resistance training as a time cue for the molecular clock mechanism in skeletal muscle. The conclusion is that resistance exercise can act as a dominant cue for setting clocks in peripheral tissues; however, much more data are needed to understand the relationship.

The results of one study (27) on the effects of resistance training on muscle clock entrainment reinforce the notion that circadian rhythms in peripheral tissues, such as muscles, can be dissociated from the master clock. These data clearly support the idea that muscle clocks respond to systematic exercise, including resistance training, reprogramming in response to consistently timed exercise (7). Peripheral clocks can use nonlight signals, such as muscle contraction, to self-regulate, providing more evidence for the emerging line of thought that muscles are autonomous regulators and not just effectors.

Provide Timing Cues to Muscle

In exercise programming, timing is everything, from the total length in months of a periodization program to the recovery time between resistance and cardiovascular exercise sessions to intraset rest breaks. Timing is critical to muscle clocks. It is clear that predictably timed daily loading and unloading of muscle associated with exercise, along with its related metabolic changes, is an important part of local muscle entrainment.

Exercise provides timing cues to muscles that are used to entrain muscle clocks and tissues to optimize performance. Successful periodization training is based on timing the exercise programming variables correctly over approximately a year to achieve peak performance at the right time. Timing is not new in exercise science, but its foundation. What is new is the idea that the timing of exercise, from the frequency of sessions to the time between sessions and sets and even intraset breaks, could function as an entrainment cue to self-regulate muscle and other tissues. The idea is relatively new but is supported by evidence showing that exercise at different times of the day can shift circadian rhythms (9).

The time of day of exercise and its frequency can influence whole body circadian rhythmicity (2). The data, although narrow, illustrate the importance of the timing of exercise in providing stability to the daily rhythms of the entire circadian system.

The time of day that rhythmic genes are most active indicates when they are responding and initiating cellular activities associated with muscle performance. The phase of expression of many rhythmic genes in skeletal muscle in rats occurs at the midpoint of the active phase (13, 14). The active phase in rats is analogous to daytime in humans. Two studies (13, 14) reported a large group of genes that peak in activity during the middle of the active phase in rats and midday in humans. Because rat activity is reflected by wheel running, these findings reinforce the idea that locomotor activity may play a role in entraining the rhythmic expression of genes in skeletal muscle. In humans, that would mean that scheduled running or jogging can change the circadian rhythm in skeletal muscles (26), and the cycle of rhythmic gene expression in skeletal muscle may be regulated by the rhythm of locomotor activity.

If exercise can shift the behavior of skeletal muscles, it is paramount to understand how. In one study (9), mice were subjected to scheduled bouts of cardiovascular exercise performed for 2 h per day in the light phase, 4 h after the lights were turned on. The important thing to note is the reference to 4 h after the lights were turned on. In humans, that would equate to 4 h after waking up. The timing of exercise relative to the time of lights on is important because previous studies have shown that in humans the time between waking and performance is critical (13, 14). Researchers (9) found a significant shift in clock gene expression in all of the three different skeletal muscles from the exercised mice, whereas the molecular clock in the SCN remained unchanged. The different expression of the skeletal muscle versus the master clock demonstrates again that scheduled exercise can alter the molecular clock in peripheral tissues without affecting the master clock. This is yet another study that supports the autonomy of skeletal muscle.

Finally, one study (26) showed that the effects of exercise on phase shifting muscle clocks depend on the specific muscle. In the flexor digitorum brevis (finger muscle), the circadian phase advanced more than in either the soleus (lower, outside leg muscle) and extensor digitorum longus (finger muscle), suggesting the potential for differential regulation of the molecular clock in individual muscles.

Create Muscle Anticipation

The ability of skeletal muscle to anticipate changes in the environment and make the necessary cellular alterations in advance of anticipated changes is one of the most important aspects of the discovery of muscle clocks. The body of work supporting muscle anticipation is limited but promising. One study examined the ability of muscles in schedule-trained horses to anticipate upcoming training sessions (15). The results showed that the peak expression of uncoupling protein 3 (UCP3), a factor critical to the synthesis of ATP into energy, preceded the regularly scheduled time of exercise. These data showed muscles anticipated exercise training and, as a direct result, stimulated the antioxidant response that is otherwise produced during exercise. By anticipation, UCP3 expression increased right before scheduled exercise, thus generating sufficient UCP3 to cope with exercise, when oxidative stress, an imbalance between free radicals and antioxidants, is maximal.

These findings fundamentally support the notion that muscles anticipate exercise training. They show that muscles are able to prepare for upcoming scheduled training and click on the associated mechanisms of muscle performance before the exercise begins. This discovery suggests an anticipatory process in muscles, which would support the idea that timing of resistance training allows muscles the luxury to better prepare ahead of training.

Although the data from the Murphy study (15) were collected on schedule-trained horses, the results can cautiously be applied to humans. One study (23) set out to determine if the time of day of training corresponded to an improvement in performance. Participants were assigned to a morning (7 to 8 a.m.) or evening (7 to 8 p.m.) training group. Both groups completed four tests that measured strength and power: unilateral isometric maximal voluntary knee extension, squat-jump, countermovement jump, and Wingate tests. All tests were performed at 7 a.m. and 7 p.m. before and after 6 weeks of resistance training. The resistance training was done 2 days per week with at least 48 h between sessions. Each session included 2 sets of 10 repetitions of bench press, hack squat, leg extension, leg curl, and machine pullover. All exercises were done at 50% 1RM during the first 2 weeks of training and 60% 1RM during the last 4 weeks. Participants were allowed a 2 min rest between each set and a 3 min rest between each of the five exercises. The results of the study indicate that the best performances are obtained at the same time of the day as the scheduled training, indicating there is some type of timed anticipatory mechanisms in humans as well.

The Souissi and coworkers study (23) on muscle anticipation is promising. However, a note of caution is warranted when applying the results of the study to adults with resistance training experience, because untrained children were used as the research subjects. Further research in the area will shed light on the presence of muscle anticipation in trained athletes and the relationships between timing of resistance training and optimal performance.

Enhance Individual Chronotype

Exercise exerts influence over the molecular clock in skeletal muscle, and the clock modulates the physiological activity of skeletal tissue, causing the muscle to phase shift and reset to the regularly scheduled exercise. However, one thing to always bear in mind with exercise training is *chronotype*, or individual variability among people. Individual chronotype affects training effectiveness, safety, and outcomes. This section covers a few biological similarities across all people but focuses on individual chronotype, or each person's individual natural predisposition for sleep–wake patterns and time of day when he or she is most alert and performs best.

Some things, such as peak testosterone levels, are similar across all people. Testosterone levels are highest in the morning and begin to decrease in late afternoon to reach their lowest point in the late evening. Body temperature, on the other hand, peaks between 4 and 6 p.m. and is believed to be a leading contributor to why muscle strength, speed, and pliability also peak between 4 and 6 p.m. for most people.

On the other hand, muscle endurance and stamina peak early to mid-morning, and mental acuity peaks around midday. Therefore, cardiovascular training is typically most effective in the early to mid-morning and sport-specific training is most effective around midday.

Muscles are monitoring hormone levels, tissue pliability, and other things unique to each person, such as sleeping and eating patterns and time of day when the person is most alert. For example, the chronotype for those described as night people indicates that they are most alert in the late evening and even well into the night. Alertness depends on chronotype and can affect clock entrainment and training effectiveness. Along with the physiological changes in testosterone levels, which are stable across most people, being aware of individual activity–rest and eating patterns will help when designing the most effective resistance training program.

In support of the relevance of chronotypes to resistance training programs, a study (10) showed the importance of considering the athlete's chronotype, based on sleep-onset time, sleep duration, and wake-up time, when determining the time of optimal performance. The study was done by classifying participants into one of three circadian chronotype groups—early, intermediate, and late—based on a novel questionnaire that examined sleep–wake patterns. Athletes were then asked to perform the beep fitness assessment, a progressive aerobic cardiovascular endurance test to estimate maximum oxygen uptake. The tests were performed at six different times in one day. The findings showed that the highest performances were obtained at different times of the day, depending on the individual chronotype. For example, the early circadian chronotype group performed best around noon. As suspected, the results were different for the later chronotype groups. The intermediate circadian chronotype group performance peaked around 6 p.m., and the late circadian chronotype group performed best at 9 p.m. These results highlight the importance of individual chronobiology in skeletal muscle activity. Planning training and competition at the right time is essential for optimal improvement of skeletal muscle performance (10).

It is well established that the time of day is important regarding skeletal muscle performance. In humans, more than 20 studies have shown that skeletal muscle torque, strength, and power are higher in the late afternoon, between 4 and 6 p.m., compared to the morning (28). It is important to note that the skeletal muscle cycles are more related to daily cycles of the tissue itself than to neural factors such as fatigue (22).

Conclusion

Muscle tissue is highly adaptable. Muscle mass adapts to different conditions through regulation of pathways responsible for protein synthesis and cellular activity. External stimuli, such as scheduled resistance training, can increase the rate of muscle protein synthesis and result in positive muscle changes, including increased hypertrophy, strength, and speed. Emerging data continue to make the case for the autonomy of muscles and the role of muscle in whole body rhythms. This makes perfect sense given that muscle is the single most abundant tissue in the human body. The notion that muscle is simply an effector under central nervous system command no longer holds up. Muscles are both intelligent and autonomous, as demonstrated by the presence of independent muscle clocks with an array of unique genes that express themselves in accordance with their environment and scheduled resistance training. In addition, muscles have the ability to anticipate upcoming training and click on the desired molecular responses associated with muscle performance outcomes.

2 Overcoming Chaos, Confusion, and Interference

Resistance training and cardiovascular training are competing modes of exercise that initiate different muscle molecular actions. When cardiovascular and resistance training are performed within a single session or even within the same day, muscle performance can be adversely affected. This chapter examines interference theory and its mechanisms and explores ways to develop resistance training workouts and programs to avoid it.

Molecular Competition

Most athletes and fitness enthusiasts do *concurrent training*, or resistance and cardiovascular training in the same session or day, to achieve multiple training goals. Concurrent training is defined as doing some form of resistance training along with cardiovascular training, such as jogging, cycling, or sprint intervals, in the same workout session or program. In athletics and fitness, concurrent training is necessary for achieving all aspects of conditioning and optimal performance. But the question most athletes, fitness enthusiasts, athletic and personal trainers, strength and sport coaches, and research scientists continue to ask is, Does concurrent training achieve multiple goals, or is it counterproductive?

The answer seems to lie in the fact that muscles are intelligent. Muscles know the difference between resistance and cardiovascular endurance training. They also know the difference between two unlike exercises for the same muscles, like a squat versus a lunge. Just as muscles can distinguish between types of training and exercises, they also recognize different exercise intensities such as a regular push-up versus a plyometric push-up.

Muscles are smart and recognize different training conditions such as mode, frequency, volume, and intensity. However, they crave consistency. They use their internal muscle clocks (discussed in chapter 1) to help them find consistency. Muscle clocks help muscles find cues about the time of day and type of training based on scheduled exercise programming. Muscles look for the cues from training conditions to determine how to respond by clicking on the molecular mechanisms responsible either for aerobic endurance or for hypertrophy, strength, or power improvements. Resistance and cardiovascular endurance training outcomes are mediated by different molecular actions. When training is chaotic or poorly designed, muscles get confused. They do not know which actions to activate. They shut down, and all outcomes are adversely affected. The mechanisms of aerobic endurance and strength improvements compete, diminishing the positive effects of training.

Under chaotic, unscheduled training conditions, muscles cannot anticipate what will be required of them. If resistance training is done at 11 a.m. one day and randomly at 6 p.m. a couple of days later and then at 8 a.m. later that week, muscles cannot use their internal 24 h clocks to anticipate what's next. They do not know when they should ready the molecular actions associated with muscle hypertrophy, strength, and power versus aerobic endurance outcomes.

Interference Theory

Molecular competition is studied in the context of interference theory. Interference theory is the scientifically backed idea that the long-term physiological adaptations associated with muscle growth, strength, and power versus aerobic endurance outcomes compete during individual workout sessions and over time. Thus it can be counterproductive to train for cardiovascular endurance and muscle hypertrophy, strength, and power within the same training session or even the same day.

The notion of interference dates back to 1980 when Dr. Robert Hickson first examined the competing effects of performing aerobic exercise and resistance training in the same session. The results of that first study on interference showed that when aerobic exercise and resistance training were done together over a 10-week period, both modes at high intensities and volumes, leg strength suffered (11).

Since 1980, research methods that examine interference theory have advanced significantly. However, the overall picture has been consistent with the observation that concurrent training negatively affects muscle hypertrophy, strength, and power.

Cardiovascular Endurance Training

Cardiovascular endurance training is an independent variable used in molecular competition, muscle confusion, and interference theory research. To understand the research and data on concurrent training, it is essential operationally to define *cardiovascular endurance training*. For the purposes of this chapter, cardiovascular endurance training is aerobic or anaerobic training designed to improve the performance of both the cardiovascular system and the muscles. Throughout the literature on concurrent training, cardiovascular training methods vary widely from 20 to 80 min of continuous training (CT) to short bursts of high-intensity interval training (HIIT).

Muscular Endurance

Cardiovascular endurance is defined as the ability of a muscle or muscle group to maintain repeated contractions against resistance. Muscle endurance is a key concept for understanding and applying the data on molecular competition, muscle confusion, and interference theory. Muscle endurance is vital to athletic performance and fitness success. A muscle with a high capacity for aerobic endurance can sustain repeated contractions for an extended time.

Muscle endurance is typically a product of cardiovascular or aerobic training; however, high-repetition resistance training methods also contribute to muscle endurance. In either case, the question remains, Can that same aerobic endurance–trained muscle produce strength and power when needed? The answer appears to depend on how cardiovascular endurance training is scheduled with resistance training. This is the focus of the remainder of the chapter.

Muscle Activation Patterns

Years ago in the exercise science and training world, muscle confusion was promoted as intrasession and intersession cross-training, meaning that different types of exercises, such as jogging and cycling, were performed during one session or different sessions to change the movements and muscles used. Although cross-training is a great way to take pressure off overused joints and muscles, prevent overuse injuries, and work muscles in more than one way, it is not the scientific equivalent to what is meant by the term *muscle confusion*. Nor is muscle confusion doing different exercises in quick sequence within a session to "confuse" muscles.

Muscle confusion is interference theory at a microscopic level. It is the molecular explanation for why concurrent training interferes with resistance training. Remember that muscles are intelligent, and they get confused just like a person does. Consider this example: If an athlete walks into an advanced training facility ready to do powerlifting but the gym floor is covered in yoga mats, he gets confused. The athlete does not know what to do. Muscles are the same way. When two competing modes of exercise, such as resistance and cardiovascular endurance training, are done within 30 min of each other, muscles become confused at the molecular level. Because the changes associated with resistance and endurance improvements are different, muscles simply do not know what to do. In the end, interference sets in and results are diminished.

Although it is known that concurrent training competes at the cellular level, it is still important that muscles are trained in a variety of ways. In this case, the focus is on using different exercise biomechanics instead of different modes of exercise to vary the workload. Biomechanically similar exercises work the same or similar muscles, but they activate those muscles in different ways. Different movement patterns use different bundles of muscle fibers within the same muscle. For example, both a back squat and leg press train the muscles of the legs and hips. However, each exercise activates slightly different bundles of muscle fibers within the same muscles. The end programming result is a more comprehensive workout for the entire muscle group.

To fully differentiate the popular use of the term *muscle confusion* from *interference theory*, it is important to understand the concept of the order of muscle activation. The order of muscle activation is the

1. order individual muscles within a muscle group are activated during an exercise. For example, during a leg press exercise, the muscles of the hip activate before the muscles of the knees to start the movement.
2. order muscle fiber bundles within a muscle are activated during an exercise. Individual muscle fibers within a muscle are activated differently for different exercises.

The order of deactivation, or release from contraction, varies among muscles during different exercises as well. Deactivation is determined by how long a muscle is used or contracted during an exercise.

Biomechanically similar exercises use unique orders of muscle and muscle fiber recruitment. Hence different exercises that look mechanically similar and work the same or similar muscles or muscle groups work muscles differently.

Muscle fibers within a muscle are recruited in the order from slow twitch (endurance fibers) to fast twitch (hypertrophy, strength, and power fibers). In general, the faster the movement and the more strength required to complete the movement, the more fast-twitch fibers are used. In many movements, such as walking, fast-twitch fibers are minimally involved. However, a box jump and a heavy loaded front squat recruit many fast-twitch fibers. Factors that determine muscle fiber recruitment and release order are the mechanics of the exercise, intensity (the weight, the speed of contraction, or both), and range of motion.

For example, a traditional back squat with no weight recruits fewer fast-twitch fibers overall than a loaded squat, even though the mechanics are the same. When external weight is added, increasing the intensity of the exercise, a greater number of fast-twitch fibers are recruited. They also are released later in the sequence to sustain forceful contraction throughout the entire range of motion to keep the athlete from getting stuck at the bottom of the movement.

Competing Muscle Adaptations

It is widely accepted that the long-term muscle adaptations associated with resistance versus cardiovascular endurance training compete during sessions. Both historical and contemporary data support the conclusion that the direction of interference is that cardiovascular endurance training adversely affects muscle hypertrophy, strength, and power goals (figure 2.1) (3-6, 10, 20). As science continues to evolve and examine the interference phenomenon, suggested mechanisms have emerged, including short-term chemical changes, long-term changes in muscle structure or morphology, and changes in metabolic or biochemical processes. Mechanisms of interference are discussed in detail later in the chapter.

Before the mechanisms of interference can be understood, it is essential to be familiar with the research methods used to uncover them. The first thing to recognize is that molecular competition is more likely to be seen if results are analyzed over time instead of for only one training session. This difference is critical because the original data collected by Hickson in 1980 on concurrent training focused on the effects of a single training session. This early study set out to determine if concurrent resistance and cardiovascular exercise mechanisms competed within minutes. One of the original goals was to isolate the short-term muscle changes that occurred within 1 to 1.5 h of concurrent training that caused interference. This strategy made sense early on because the objective was to determine what was going on within one session before moving on to long-term programming adaptations.

In contrast, contemporary interest in the effects of concurrent endurance and resistance training on hypertrophy, strength, and power has shifted to results after days, weeks, or even months. The reason is that long-term data are more applicable to periodization training, athletic performance, and elite fitness programming than are the results of a single session.

Competing long-term adaptions

Long-duration aerobic endurance training

Resistance training

Sprint intervals

FIGURE 2.1 Competing long-term muscle adaptations and mechanisms of interference among resistance training, long-duration aerobic endurance training, and sprint intervals.
Based on Wilson et al. (2012).

Cardiovascular Training Interferes With Resistance Training

Based on a large body of work dating back to the original Hickson study in 1980 (11) and summarized by Wilson et al. (20), the widely accepted conclusion is that cardiovascular exercise reduces the quality of resistance training sessions. Therefore, concurrent cardiovascular and resistance training reduces the likelihood of muscle growth, strength, and power improvements (table 2.1).

TABLE 2.1   Dose–Response Effect Size of Long-Duration Aerobic Endurance Training on Hypertrophy, Strength, and Power Development

Cardiovascular endurance training	EFFECT SIZE*		
	Hypertrophy	Strength	Power
1 day/week	1.2	1.7	0.9
3 days/week	0.8	1.1	0.3
5 days/week	0.5	0.4	N/A

*The lower the number, the greater the negative effect cardiovascular endurance training has on hypertrophy, strength, and power.

Based on data from J.M. Wilson et al. (2012).

Muscle hypertrophy, strength, and power outcomes are adversely affected by poorly constructed concurrent training programs. However, muscle endurance and hypertrophy, strength, and power are all primary intended outcomes of any well-rounded training program. They are also all essential aspects of performance. It is impossible to train for strength if a muscle cannot endure a forceful sustained or repeated contraction.

The idea that concurrent training negatively affects resistance training goals is critical to the timing of resistance training programs. The molecular mechanisms associated with interference are time dependent. Hickson's original study on interference showed that concurrent cardiovascular training reduces strength gains. Those data were correlated with evidence showing the molecular mechanisms responsible for strength improvements need a minimum of 3 h to reset (12). So doing cardiovascular and resistance training within the same session or even within the same 3 h is counterproductive. Concurrent training causes confusion and interference. An additional study showed molecular mechanisms need closer to 6 h and up to 24 h to fully reset and avoid interference (17). Such research shows that when cardiovascular training and resistance training occur too close together, muscle hypertrophy, strength, and power outcomes are reduced.

Muscle Force Generation Capacity

The effects of concurrent training on muscle strength and power are studied using muscle force generation capacity (MFGC). MFGC is a direct measurement of muscle strength. Because power is the product of strength and velocity or speed, MFGC also serves as a tool for determining the effects of cardiovascular training on power. The bottom line is that researchers use MFGC to measure if concurrent training is undermining strength or power improvements and to what degree.

Strength Outcomes Adversely Affected

Strength outcomes are negatively affected by concurrent training; however, muscle power is most adversely affected by concurrent training. Historical data provide the foundation for the accepted theory that cardiovascular training works against muscle strength (4), and contemporary studies continue to support that notion (5, 12). When MFGC was analyzed over a 4-day test period using combined high-intensity lower-body strength exercises with cardiovascular training, strength was diminished (5). More significant to athletics and elite fitness enthusiasts is that muscle power was diminished with only two or three low-volume cardiovascular exercise sessions per week (10, 15).

It is clear that combined cardiovascular and resistance training can reduce the likelihood of improvements in muscle hypertrophy, strength, and power. This creates a serious dilemma in athletic performance training. However, new research on timing-dependent competing mechanisms shows that strategic programming can help avoid interference.

Competing Mechanisms

At the core of all exercise programs are training variables, which are manipulated over time. Borrowing from classical periodization training, coaches and trainers modify these variables, through time and relative to one another, to create a program to reach an end goal. Programming variables are discussed here within the context of timing concurrent training for peak performance. Variables are addressed in relation to the molecular actions they activate in muscles relative to time. Analyzed variables include frequency, duration, and scheduled rest (or recovery). Variables are discussed within the context of volume of cardiovascular training. Volume, defined as the combined frequency and duration of cardiovascular training over weeks or months, is the critical factor for avoiding interference.

Frequency

The frequency of training is how often a mode of exercise is done. Frequency is commonly reflected as the number of days per week. It can also be the number of sessions within a day, if more than one session per 24 h period is warranted. Remember the muscle clocks, along with the master clock, put muscles on a 24 h schedule. They are monitoring the frequency of training events within each 24 h period to anticipate a schedule. Determining a schedule tells the clocks when to be ready to click on molecular actions associated with cardiovascular endurance or resistance training outcomes or even rest.

The frequency and volume of each type of training are both significant programming factors, but the frequency of cardiovascular training appears to be the most important factor in avoiding interference (20). However, it is not the frequency of cardiovascular exercise alone that makes the difference. It is the frequency of each mode (cardiovascular and resistance) relative to the other that is important.

The frequency of cardiovascular training relative to resistance training is often overlooked. The unfortunate assumption is that if the two types of training are done during different sessions, the timing is fine and the competing mechanisms will not kick in; however, this is not true. To successfully avoid interference, specific timing requirements must be met. When training more than once per 24 h period, guidelines suggest a minimum of 3 h rest after any workout before beginning another workout and at least 6 h, up to 24 h, rest between cardiovascular endurance training and resistance training (19).

Duration

The duration of training can be reflected in the length of the total program, individual session, or each session component (i.e., cardiovascular or resistance training). The duration of a training session combined with its frequency determines its overall volume. The volume of cardiovascular training is a significant factor in determining the extent of interference with resistance training outcomes. As a rule, cardiovascular training duration should be kept to 20 to 40 min to avoid interfering with muscle hypertrophy, strength, and power gains (12, 16, 20).

Recovery

The frequency of training accounts for active days. It also accounts for recovery days and activity–rest cycles. Remember that muscle clocks monitor activity–rest cycles, and they are looking for cues to know when to click on the molecular mechanisms associated with training outcomes or rest and recovery.

Strategic exercise programming accounts for periods of rest and recovery. Muscles must recover between training sessions to perform their best during training. Scheduled rest is essential to programming for optimal results and preventing overtraining. If there is too little rest, muscles do not adequately repair postsession, results will be minimal, and injury can result. However, if there is too much rest, detraining can occur.

General guidelines suggest that muscles need about 48 h of rest after high-intensity resistance training (anything above 80% 1RM) to recover to baseline strength (5). However, too much rest is a bad thing. Rest periods should not exceed 96 h, because after that the physiological processes of detraining begin (2).

Active recovery is suggested as a programming and exercise training tool. It provides muscle clocks with consistent activity–rest cues and includes rhythmic aerobic activities such as low-intensity cardiovascular exercise, non-weight-bearing exercise such as swimming, and short-duration high-intensity endurance training.

Interference Mechanisms

Although it is well documented that the long-term adaptations of cardiovascular training interfere with hypertrophy, strength, and power outcomes during concurrent training, less is known about what those mechanisms are and why they compete. Research is ongoing and has uncovered potential explanations for interference, categorized as structural or metabolic or both. Mechanisms include muscle contractility (metabolic), delayed-onset muscle soreness (structural and metabolic), testosterone levels (metabolic), and cortisol and blood lactate levels (metabolic).

Muscle Contractility

Prolonged cardiovascular exercise interferes with a muscle's ability to contract. Decreased contractility decreases the likelihood of positive muscle growth, strength, and power outcomes. Therefore, both the frequency and duration of cardiovascular endurance training are critical to performance outcomes.

Muscle contractility is the first and most obvious explanation for interference theory. Prolonged cardiovascular training, such as jogging, can adversely affect a muscle's ability to contract efficiently. Reduced contraction capabilities work against strength increases (4). This observation undoubtedly supports the idea that when resistance training is done after cardiovascular training, strength is adversely affected.

But muscle contractility is also affected by the length of recovery time, the intensity of each mode of exercise, and the frequency and volume of cardiovascular training. In other words, research shows that strategic programming can control contractility as a possible competing mechanism, so other factors must be in play.

Delayed-Onset Muscle Soreness

Another structural explanation for interference is delayed-onset muscle soreness (DOMS). DOMS causes a series of events, including microscopic damage to muscle fibers, that prevent strength increases. One study showed that when DOMS occurs, strength decreases over the same time that beginning exercisers have soreness (1). DOMS causes structural damage to muscles, negatively affecting muscle strength; however, it is important to note the subjects used in the referenced study were new to exercise (1). Applications to athletes and highly fit individuals accustomed to training should be made with caution, because the differences in short- and long-term adaptations to training between untrained and trained individuals are well documented.

Fitness level aside, it is reasonable to assume that anyone experiencing DOMS has sustained microscopic damage to muscle fibers. Any damage to muscle fibers might have a negative effect on the muscle's ability to contract optimally and yield strength improvements.

Contractility is one issue with DOMS, but there are also metabolic factors contributing to interference, such as substrate depletion and increased protein breakdown (4, 6). Substrate depletion is the reduced availability of adenosine triphosphate (ATP), phosphocreatine (PCr), muscle glycogen, and blood glucose. The depletion of these substrates compromises muscle functions during training and adversely affects muscle hypertrophy, strength, and power improvements.

Protein breakdown during prolonged muscle work also causes DOMS and reduces the efficacy of strength training. However, the more obvious dilemma is that protein is needed to build muscle. Therefore, when protein is depleted, hypertrophy, strength, and power performance are adversely impacted.

Testosterone Levels

Testosterone levels are another potential explanation for interference. Testosterone levels are critically necessary for muscle hypertrophy, strength, and power increases.

To determine how concurrent training affects testosterone levels, researchers measured testosterone concentrations during three different modes of training (16): strength training only, concurrent training (both cardiovascular and strength), or cardiovascular training only. The major finding was that testosterone levels increased in the strength only group. As expected, testosterone levels decreased in both the cardiovascular only and concurrent training groups.

Testosterone levels are directly related to muscle growth, strength, and power outcomes. The greater the testosterone level, the greater the muscle growth, strength, and power improvements. Therefore if concurrent training reduces testosterone levels, it can clearly decrease the effectiveness of strength training workouts both short term and long term. These decrements would then lead to long-term performance declines during training and competition. The fact that testosterone levels decreased in concurrent training is a very important finding with far-reaching implications for programming when muscle growth and strength and power improvements are goals.

Cortisol and Blood Lactate Levels

Blood lactate and cortisol levels are additional metabolic factors that determine the efficacy (or lack thereof) of concurrent training. Where it is desirable that testosterone levels be high to yield muscle hypertrophy, strength, and power improvements, the opposite is true of blood lactate and cortisol concentrations. These levels should be low, or they interfere with increases in muscle and strength.

A recent study looked at the effects of concurrent training on MFGC and testosterone, cortisol, and lactate blood concentrations in recreational athletes (12), and the results are important to the current understanding of the behavior of competing mechanisms during concurrent training. Researchers compared strength training only to strength training before cardiovascular training and cardiovascular training before strength training. Note that the training order was studied, not just the presence of concurrent training. The study showed that testosterone increased in all three training conditions, contrary to previously collected data (16). Not surprising, MFGC was adversely affected when cardiovascular training was done before strength training, most likely a direct result of decreased contractility.

The new finding was that blood lactate and cortisol levels were elevated when cardiovascular training was done before strength training. The bottom line is this: Doing cardiovascular exercise before strength training within the same session reduces muscle force. Cardiovascular training before strength training also interferes with muscle hypertrophy, strength, and power by elevating blood lactate and cortisol levels, which interfere with molecular adaptations associated with the desired performance outcomes.

Avoiding Interference

It is clear that interference happens, and that cardiovascular training gets in the way of muscle hypertrophy, strength, and power improvements. The problem is that both cardiovascular and muscle endurance are required for conditioning. The solution lies in the strategic use of mode, frequency, and duration of cardiovascular exercise relative to resistance training. The remainder of this chapter focuses on specific programming solutions to combat interference and maximize performance.

Frequency

Resistance and cardiovascular training need to be scheduled differently to avoid interference. If a program includes strength and cardiovascular endurance goals, it is best to schedule each mode of exercise on alternate days (5). That does not just mean doing resistance and cardiovascular training on different days and the problem is solved. Alternating days is only the beginning of the programming puzzle. It is a good start and an easy programming suggestion, but, when the data are examined closely, the suggested frequency of each mode of training is more complex.

Resistance Training

Although the frequency of cardiovascular training is a determinant of interference, the frequency of resistance training should be taken into account as well. Resistance training should be done 2 or 3 days per week. The intensity of sessions and the training split—which muscles are worked on which days—also are factors. A well-defined split of 3 to 5 days a week is consistent with data that show increasing the frequency of resistance training does not improve strength (8). It is also consistent with a well-defined training program that accounts for incorporating 48 h rest between high-intensity (>80% 1 RM) resistance training sessions for the same muscles (5).

Cardiovascular Training

The frequency of cardiovascular training is one of the main culprits for interference theory. Programming suggestions are to limit cardiovascular exercise frequency to less than 3 days per week to minimize the effects on strength (20). Duration of cardiovascular training should not exceed 40 min (16). However, more conservative estimates suggest keeping cardiovascular training volume at no more than 20 min, with 30 min maximum (20).

The type of cardiovascular exercise is critical to influencing the degree that cardiovascular training affects hypertrophy, strength, and power outcomes. Research shows that jogging or running has a greater negative effect on muscle contractility and thus more influence over resistance training outcomes than cycling (17, 20). Therefore, cycling is recommended for concurrent training programs instead of jogging or running.

It is easy to suggest cycling as a programming solution, but it is important to understand why it works well with concurrent training and contributes to muscle hypertrophy. The simple explanation is that cycling does not include eccentric action, which is known to cause more microscopic damage to muscle fibers, and hence could contribute more to interference during resistance training, than concentric contraction. In addition to the absence of eccentric contraction, cycling loads muscles in a manner similar to resistance training. The mechanical resistance from the parts of the bike during peddling can act like an external weight. Pushing a big gear is like doing a heavy-weight lunge.

Volume

The volume of cardiovascular training—how often (frequency) and how long (duration)—appears to determine the degree to which cardiovascular training interferes with resistance training. The amount of time spent in cardiovascular training affects muscle contractility and thus influences the force that a muscle can produce. To minimize the negative effects of cardiovascular training on performance outcomes, the recommendation is that cardiovascular training last 20 to 30 min only (20). However, up to 40 min of low-intensity cardiovascular training is acceptable (17).

Intensity

The variation in the volume of cardiovascular training is influenced by its intensity. Lower intensities of exercise are associated with longer durations. What is important to resistance training outcomes is that the extent of muscle force impairment is directly related to the intensity of the endurance training (5). Specifically, moderate- to high-intensity cardiovascular training reduced the effectiveness of strength training. Therefore, the suggested intensity of cardiovascular sessions should be low (40% to 50% maximum heart rate) if hypertrophy, strength, and power are primary training goals (5).

Practical considerations and training goals will influence the utility of low-intensity cardiovascular training sessions. The key for each practitioner is to decide if low- to moderate-intensity endurance sessions are enough to reach the overall program goals. The periodic frequency of moderate- to high-intensity sessions might be warranted and should be considered on a case-by-case basis and timed in accordance with the guidelines on rest and recovery periods.

Recovery Between Competing Modes of Exercise

Intracellular competition peaks when resistance and endurance training are done within 30 min of one another (4, 17). This is when interference is at its greatest, and hypertrophy, strength, and power increases are not likely achievable.

When resistance and endurance bouts are separated by 6 h or more, whole muscle growth is greater in the concurrent training group versus the resistance training only group (17). When 24 h rest is given between training bouts, whole muscle size doubles, suggesting that it is not concurrent training that causes interference but the timing of the two modes relative to one another as suspected by the discovery of muscle clocks.

Whole muscle hypertrophy is a crude performance measurement, and thus caution is advised when interpreting these findings. However, the data are significant in that they show rudimentary evidence of the value of timing of resistance training.

Baseline Strength Recovery

Muscles need 48 h for baseline strength to recover after a high-intensity strength training session. This finding is based on data collected from knee extensor torque (KET), which showed that KET and MFGC were compromised up to 2 days after high-intensity strength training (5). The data show that after strength training at a high intensity (typically defined as ≥80% 1RM), an athlete requires 48 h rest for full recovery (5). Therefore, considering resistance training outcomes only, it is best to use an alternate day schedule for high-intensity strength training.

High-Intensity Interval Training

Continuous endurance training interferes with muscle hypertrophy, strength, and power. Historical data showed this phenomenon nearly 40 years ago. However, it was shown using continuous training aerobic sessions at an average intensity of 70% $\dot{V}O_2$max up to 70 min in duration! The results are not surprising based on current knowledge about contractility alone; 70 min of CT would negatively affect muscle's ability to contract. It would also deplete vital substrates necessary for both contraction and catabolic events.

Although CT has its place in sports and fitness, the industry evolved and, with it, HIIT or short-interval, high-intensity endurance training emerged at the forefront of training methods. Logically, researchers started to ask if HIIT would have the same effect on muscle performance outcomes during concurrent training as CT.

As a training tool, HIIT is undeniably effective for improving endurance. It also improves muscle hypertrophy because it preferentially uses fast-twitch muscle fibers. It sounded like a great solution to concurrent programming for hypertrophy, strength, and power goals. The research questions became, Is it an effective way to avoid interference? Can HIIT be used to train for endurance while avoiding mass, strength, and power decrements?

The assumption is logical. HIIT uses short-duration, high-intensity intervals to improve cardiovascular stamina. Because historical and contemporary data continue to expose high-volume endurance training as the cause of interference, HIIT should work as a solution to concurrent programming.

However, the answer is not that simple. The hypothesis that HIIT would not interfere with resistance training outcomes was not supported. When HIIT was done before resistance training, muscle force was reduced (3). Unfortunately, the high-intensity training fatigued muscles, reducing muscle force and resistance training volume.

However, subsequent data are more promising for HIIT as a programming solution to interference. A current study shows that longer-duration cardiovascular endurance training is more adverse than shorter-duration, high-intensity endurance sessions on muscle mass, strength, and power outcomes (7). The current position is that HIIT, not CT, should be used with concurrent programs because training volume seems to affect muscle hypertrophy, strength, and power more than intensity.

Upper- Versus Lower-Body Training

Most of the data collected on the effects of concurrent training on muscle strength analyzed lower-body strength. In most cases, a 1RM squat is used to measure lower-body strength. However, one study examined the effects of lower-body sprint interval training on upper-body hypertrophy and strength (13). Results showed that sprint interval training combined with resistance training adversely affected upper-body hypertrophy and strength. This finding is interesting because it shows that the effects of concurrent aerobic endurance and resistance training are not muscle-use specific. Lower-body sprint interval training had a negative effect on upper-body strength performance. The results showed that the effects of endurance training influence nonworking muscles. Hence, the data demonstrated that the mechanisms responsible for interference cannot be avoided by using different muscle groups for aerobic endurance and strength training.

Resistance-Trained Athletes

Research has clearly demonstrated that resistance training should be done before cardiovascular training to avoid interference. This programming strategy applies to both HIIT and CT when they are done in the same session as resistance training or within 3 h of one another.

However, the story looks a little different when subjects have a history of resistance training. Serious athletes respond differently to concurrent training protocols than do recreational athletes or moderately trained and untrained individuals. For conditioned ice hockey and rugby players, concurrent training under both HIIT (8 to 24 short-duration intervals at 150% $\dot{V}O_2max$) and CT (40 to 80 min at 70% $\dot{V}O_2max$) conditions resulted in strength improvements (18). This 2018 study showed that lower-body maximal strength, as measured by parallel squat improvement, increased when cardiovascular training is done after resistance training. The resistance training protocol included 2 to 6 sets of heavy parallel squats. Heavy was defined as >80% of 1RM. The intervention period lasted 6 weeks, and each session was done 3 days per week. The magnitude of strength improvement was not influenced by the type of cardiovascular training—HIIT or CT—arguing against data that suggest interference occurs because high-volume or high-intensity cardiovascular training reduces the effectiveness of resistance training. At least in highly conditioned athletes, this was not the finding. However, again, the answer might lie in the different subjects and differential responses to resistance training based on experience versus an across-the-board mechanism.

Strength improved in conditioned athletes with concurrent training. However, there were no improvements in power when resistance training was done in combination with either HIIT or CT (18). This could be because resistance training was done to muscle failure. It is recognized that power gains are optimally achieved through subfailure paradigms. Training to failure could be the reason strength improved while power did not, not the presence of resistance training.

Another important consideration of the study is that HIIT improved $\dot{V}O_2$max but CT did not (18). HIIT is more time efficient overall than CT and is most likely a better programming choice for athletics. One of the reasons HIIT is more beneficial to muscle performance during concurrent training is because it uses fast- versus slow-twitch fibers. HIIT along with moderate- to high-intensity resistance training essentially double-loads the fast-twitch fibers associated with growth, strength, and power outcomes.

High-Intensity Interval Training, Sleep, and Athletes

Any discussion of HIIT and performance requires at least a mention of sleep. Restorative sleep is recovery. It is vital to well-being, physical and mental health, cognition, recuperation of muscles, and muscle growth. But the catch is HIIT is known to cause sleep disturbances. When Gupta and colleagues (9) reviewed more than 1,600 studies designed to determine the quality of sleep among athletes, athletes who performed HIIT were shown to have longer sleep latencies (transition times), increased sleep fragmentation (cannot stay asleep), nonrestorative sleep (still tired after sleeping), and excessive daytime fatigue. HIIT is a recognized contributor to sleep disturbances and thus performance decrements in athletes (9).

The back-and-forth relationship between sleep and exercise is an interesting dilemma. Low- to moderate-intensity exercise with the occasional high-intensity bout is vital to maintaining healthy sleep habits. This has been long known; however, scientists are just now learning that the reason is muscle clocks. Using a regularly scheduled exercise program as a tool, muscle clocks synchronize body systems associated with sleep and activity–rest cycles that ultimately enhance muscle recovery and performance outcomes. How HIIT will fit in is to be determined, but regular training schedules are a part of the solution.

Evidence From Aerobic Endurance Athletes

If cardiovascular training volume impedes resistance training, then aerobic endurance–trained athletes are at a disadvantage. Remember that cardiovascular training volume is the product of frequency and duration. Cardiovascular endurance athletes typically train frequently and for long durations.

Researchers set out to test the hypothesis that endurance athletes would not see the same muscle hypertrophy from resistance training as untrained subjects. When untrained subjects and elite aerobic endurance athletes (>10 hours per week of aerobic activity) were compared after a resistance training intervention, the untrained subjects showed double the hypertrophy of the athletes (14). The response was not due to initial baseline differences in muscle size.

A possible confounding factor is caloric intake. Aerobic endurance athletes need a lot of calories, and there might not be enough to meet the demands of both types of training adaptations. Another consideration is overtraining in long-duration aerobic endurance athletes. Overtraining causes chronic muscle soreness and delayed recovery, both of which influence muscle performance. Further studies are warranted in this area to learn if the negative effects on muscle hypertrophy are due to overtraining (high-volume cardiovascular training), interference, dietary needs, or a combination of all factors.

Time of Day

Muscle clocks are on a 24 h schedule. Many biological functions that contribute to muscle performance are also on a 24 h schedule. A closer look at these biological functions reveals that nature built in a way to avoid interference.

Consider the following observations. Aerobic endurance and stamina peak first thing in the morning. It is recognized in training circles that early to mid-morning is the best time for cardiovascular training. Cognition is greatest around midday. Midday is the best time to do sport-specific and mental training.

Testosterone levels are highest in the morning, begin to level off between 4 and 6 p.m., and then decrease after that. Muscle strength is greatest for most people between 4 and 6 p.m. Muscle speed is maximized between 4 and 6 p.m. Muscles are most pliable and produce the greatest force between 4 and 6 p.m. Taken into account, these factors suggest that strength, mass, and power training will be maximized between 4 and 6 p.m. Most serious strength athletes take advantage of these endogenous biological changes and train for hypertrophy, strength, and power during the late afternoon and early evening.

If these biological considerations are taken into account when building a concurrent training program, critical timing specifications are met automatically. The minimum 3 h rest between training sessions is met. It is possible to provide the optimal 6 to 24 h rest period between sessions.

Programming Summary

The field is packed with data on concurrent training. This summary is provided to clarify the most important programming factors when the primary training goal is to improve muscle hypotrophy, strength, and power.

Considering cardiovascular endurance training volume, frequency, intensity, and mode together, the recommendation is 2 or 3 days per week of cardiovascular training (20). Intensity should be low to moderate (40% to 50% maximum heart rate) if continuous (5). However, short-duration HIIT is recommended over continuous training because HIIT minimizes total volume (7). Sessions should last 20 to 30 min per bout (20); 20 min is adequate. Cycling is recommended over jogging or running; however, short-interval sprints can be used (17, 20).

For strength goals, combine cardiovascular endurance training with two different muscle-specific exercises 2 to 4 days per week. Include 2 to 4 sets at ≥80% 1RM. This is a reasonable recommendation for facilitating maximal hypertrophic adaptations.

Rest muscles for at least 48 h after high-intensity resistance training (>80% 1RM) (5). Do not exceed 96 h of rest or detraining occurs (2).

Conclusion

Timing of all workouts relative to one another is vital to exercise programming success. Aerobic endurance training interferes with muscle hypertrophy, strength, and power outcomes. However, the strategic timing of aerobic endurance and resistance training sessions can minimize the effects of competing mechanisms and interference. Successful periodization programming relies on deliberate timing of all workouts from the time of day aerobic endurance and resistance training workouts are scheduled to how much time is allowed between aerobic endurance and resistance training sessions. Other timing factors include how often each type of workout is scheduled to how long an exercise session lasts and within session timing variables like intraset, or within set, breaks and even the speed of muscle contractions. When these factors are taken into account, interference is minimized and muscle performance is improved.

It is well documented that the timing of workouts is critical to muscle performance, but scientists have just begun to understand how timing is monitored via newly discovered muscle clocks. Muscles clocks monitor time to help minimize interference, but, more important, muscles use the clocks to help them anticipate aerobic and endurance workouts and make adjustments ahead of exercise sessions to improve muscle performance.

PART II | LEARN THE TOOLS FOR EXERCISE PROGRAMMING

Muscle clocks learn what to expect, when, and how to respond by paying attention to consistently delivered time cues, including exercise programming and training cues. With the right time cues, muscle clocks are able to monitor 24 h daily rhythms, anticipate upcoming training sessions, and activate in advance the molecular actions associated with muscle performance and recovery.

All biological clocks reset their natural cycles in accordance with tissue-specific internal and external time cues. Resetting clocks in response to what is happening inside and outside of the body is called *phase shifting*. Phase shifting is a critical concept for understanding the significance of cues to all biological clocks. In the case of muscle clocks, a phase shift occurs when consistently delivered time cues cause a local tissue, such as muscle, to change its daily pattern. Exercise programming and training cues deliver information to muscles that help them establish their own rhythms, prepare for resistance training ahead of scheduled sessions, and learn when to expect rest and recovery.

Chapter 3 explores the types of timing cues that muscle clocks use to monitor time intervals and relates those cues to exercise program design. Muscle clocks look for three main categories of timing cues: environmental, physiological, and exercise training and programming. Within each category of cues, specific examples are provided and discussed with relevance to resistance training programming and recovery. The chapter also introduces the concept of *biomechanical similarity,* a resistance training method that pairs two exercises with similar joint and muscle actions intended to deliver consistent timing cues, optimizing muscle performance.

Successful application and use of the concept of biomechanical similarity in exercise programming and training relies on knowing which exercises use similar muscles and joint actions. The biomechanical similarity of exercises is also determined by the degree to which the exercises use overall similar motions and muscle activation patterns. Similar motions, such as a squat and a jump squat, are easy to spot, but things get a little more difficult when trying to visualize what is happening inside muscles when two similar movements are done. That is where muscle activation patterns—how individual muscle fibers and muscles within a muscle group are activated—during an exercise play a role; these patterns are explained in chapter 4.

To make exercise analyses easier, chapter 4 provides a biomechanical analysis for common exercises. Suggested exercises are categorized into six groups: all-body power, bilateral lower body, unilateral lower body, upper body, isolation, and plyometric. Plyometric exercises are further classified as bilateral lower-body exercises, unilateral lower-body exercises, and upper-body exercises. Selected exercises are broken down by the primary muscles and joint actions used, and plyometric exercises are further organized by low, medium, and high intensity.

The concept of biomechanically similar paired exercises and their muscle and joint actions are illustrated in photos in chapter 4. A limited number of paired exercise suggestions are made to introduce how to use biomechanically similar exercises to build resistance training programs for strength and power development, which is covered in more detail in chapters 7 and 8. Finally, the concept of how to build complex training programs is introduced; this information is referenced later in chapter 9.

3 Muscle Clocks' Need for Cues and Recovery

Muscle clocks rely on time cues to monitor muscle activity. Biological clocks, including muscle clocks, use time cues also termed *circadian hooks* to keep track of time intervals and as a result phase-shift. A *phase shift* occurs when a biological clock changes its daily rhythm in response to one or more consistently delivered time cues over weeks or months. By paying attention to the time cues, or circadian hooks, biological systems, including muscles, learn to coordinate their molecular actions with the external environment and internal physiological events. For example, using regularly scheduled resistance training as the cue, muscle clocks can phase-shift to activate the desired molecular actions at a specific time of day, improving muscle performance and avoiding interference, as discussed in chapter 2. Using time cues, muscle clocks learn what to expect when and how to respond. With consistent cues, muscles are able to monitor time intervals, anticipate what is next, and activate the molecular actions associated with muscle performance and recovery.

Muscle clocks actively look for a wide range of time cues that can be broken down into three main categories: environmental, physiological, and exercise training and programming. In this chapter, each cue category is discussed, including specific examples of cues provided to biological clocks, with a focus on muscle clocks. Time cues are further broken down to explain how they relate to timing a resistance training program and scheduling recovery. Note that eating patterns, discussed with physiological cues, play an important role in helping skeletal muscles synchronize to other body systems.

Light, termed *photic* in the research, is the most recognized time cue for setting and resetting biological clocks and rhythms. It is the most important zeitgeber, or circadian hook, to the master clock. The master clock receives direct light input and sends signals directly to the peripheral clocks about day–night changes based on light cues alone. Although light is the most studied cue and most widely recognized method for entraining biological clocks, scientists now know that biological clocks respond to a variety of time cues, setting and resetting their 24 h cycles in response to many different consistently delivered cues. Peripheral clocks, including muscle clocks, use light, along with multiple cues within all three cue categories, to monitor time intervals, anticipate changes in the external and internal environment, and coordinate physiological responses.

Environmental Cues

The most common cue is light, primarily from the sun, but artificial light can be used to entrain clocks in the absence of sunlight, although with less influence. Sunlight is the primary environmental cue about the position of the earth relative to the sun. In general, sunlight provides the master clock in the brain with information about the time of day during a 24 h cycle.

Whereas light is the dominant cue, darkness is also a cue. The presence of light triggers activity within cells and whole body movement, while darkness triggers the desire to rest and sleep. Both phases are critical to proper clock entrainment and the health of the organism. Both light and dark phases influence the effectiveness of resistance training by providing information about time of day relative to scheduled exercise and recovery.

Light exposure is required to reset the circadian rhythm daily. In the absence of light–dark cycles, such as in people who are totally blind and cannot process light stimulus, the circadian clock is affected, and the master clock struggles to maintain a 24 h cycle (6). Light also influences peripheral clocks, including muscle clocks, which work under the influence of the master clock. The muscle clocks use light–dark phases as one way to set their own 24 h cycles and coordinate their physiological responses to the master clock's dominant 24 h phase.

The relationship between light–dark phases is the most commonly recognized cue for setting and resetting all biological clocks, in particular the master clock. Even though the master clock is relaying information to the muscle clocks about the time of day, light–dark phases have a significant effect on muscle clocks. Muscle clocks learn a schedule by paying attention to light–dark cycles associated with activity–rest cycles. Light–dark exposure cues, along with physiological and exercise training and programming cues (discussed later), give muscle clocks the ability to activate specific molecular actions at specific times of the day.

Activity–Rest Patterns

Activity–rest patterns are partially determined by light–dark phases of a 24 h cycle. Humans tend to be more active during the day as a direct reflection of the circadian rhythm aligning itself to light–dark patterns established by the sun.

However, as discussed in chapter 1, activity–rest patterns may vary from person to person based on individual chronotype. A person's chronotype describes whether someone is a morning, midday, or night person. In addition to chronotype, social factors also influence activity–rest patterns. Social factors, such as exposure to artificial light, work and school schedules, and even having an active late-night social life (16), may contribute to a false rhythm. A false rhythm is a forced schedule and is defined by almost always requiring an alarm clock to wake up earlier than desired. Although social factors are beyond the scope of this book, it is important to recognize that biological rhythms are affected by numerous factors and that social factors are a natural part of modern life that affect muscle clocks.

Regardless of chronotype, the master clock is aware of light–dark phases and works daily to keep the body on a 24 h schedule. For most people, activity–rest patterns are coordinated to light–dark cycles by all internal clocks, including muscle clocks. Most people naturally wake up in the morning in alignment with the onset of daylight, albeit later than an alarm clock usually goes off. Along with the master clock working to maintain synchronization with light–dark phases, skeletal muscle cellular activity is naturally coordinated to the time of day as well; these muscle-specific cues are covered next in the section.

Physiological Cues

Physiological cues are biological markers inside the body that internal clocks recognize as time cues. They are biochemical changes that reflect the time of day and changes in muscle activity, such as training and rest patterns, type of scheduled exercise, and naturally fluctuating hormone levels. Physiological cues are far more numerous than environmental cues and include things such as testosterone, human growth hormone (HGH), and cortisol levels along with muscle pliability. Biochemical levels and natural patterns of highs and lows are influenced by both *endogenous* (inside the body) and *exogenous* (outside the body) factors. An example of an endogenous biological marker is the natural fluctuating testosterone levels throughout the day, while an exogenous factor is cortisol release caused by exercise.

Along with biochemical markers, muscle clocks look for specific physiological cues, such as skeletal muscle pliability, that vary with the time of day. Tissue pliability is an indication of the natural elasticity of muscle, and it varies significantly from the time someone wakes to when he or she goes to bed. In accordance with body temperature changes throughout the day, muscle tissue is least pliable first thing in the morning, but, as the day goes on, the natural elasticity of muscle increases, peaking between 4 and 6 p.m. This is important; it shows that muscles have internal time cues that provide them with a way to monitor their own natural cycles and set their own rhythms, independent of the master clock and other biological functions, such as glucose levels and eating patterns.

Testosterone

Testosterone levels naturally fluctuate throughout the day. Muscle clocks are aware of these fluctuations and account for them when setting and resetting 24 h biological rhythms. Testosterone levels are highest in the morning and begin to level off between 4 and 6 p.m, decreasing after that. The assumption is that testosterone is needed during the day and not needed for sleep. The daily fluctuation in testosterone levels is a perfect example of synchrony within the human body: Natural-occurring levels of a hormone required for muscle strength and power are highest early in the day when clocks anticipate activity and decrease ahead of anticipated rest.

Although testosterone levels naturally change throughout the day in a pattern consistent with most people, testosterone levels can be manipulated by factors such as resistance training. Resistance training influences testosterone levels during and after a workout session.

It is well known that testosterone levels climb during resistance training. When male exercisers with resistance training experience performed 3 sets of 15 repetitions of chest press, seated pec deck, lat pulldown, biceps curl, and knee extension and flexion at 60% 1RM with a 90 s rest interval between sets, blood levels of testosterone increased (17). The results showed that compared to a control day without resistance training, one bout of moderate-intensity resistance training increased testosterone levels. It is important to note that the subjects had resistance training experience and the exercises consisted of mostly isolation exercises. The effects of exercise on testosterone levels were shown in the absence of compound, large-muscle exercises such as squats and deadlifts, which are known to be an effective stimulus that increases testosterone (17).

In another study, resistance training increased resting testosterone levels 40% over a 4-week study period (1). In this study, 20 young men without prior resistance training experience performed bench press, seated pulley row, knee extension, behind the neck press, leg press, biceps curl, and triceps pulldown exercises, in that order, 3 days per week (Monday, Wednesday, and Friday). The training schedule was consistent with recommendations to alternate days between strength training. Three sets of 10 repetitions of each exercise were done at 70% to 75% 1RM. Participants were allowed 3 min of recovery between sets. The 3 days per week program of mostly isolation exercises was enough to significantly increase testosterone levels over 1 month in novice weightlifters.

Additional research has shown that testosterone levels remain elevated up to 30 min after resistance training (8). Elevated testosterone levels during and after resistance training illustrate the value of regularly scheduled resistance training to set muscle clocks. Muscle clocks monitor cues such as testosterone levels within a 24 h period, so regularly scheduled resistance training that releases testosterone into the bloodstream will cue skeletal muscles and other tissues that resistance training occurs at that time of day, and muscles will prepare ahead of it.

More specific than resistance training only, testosterone levels respond differently to different exercises, such as the squat versus the dumbbell curl (figure 3.1). The exercises used in the studies described (1, 8) were interesting because they were not those typically associated with the largest hormonal increases, which stimulate muscle growth and ultimately strength and power improvements. For example, a squat, an all-body exercise and stressor, releases more testosterone into the bloodstream than does a dumbbell curl, an isolation exercise using one joint and small arm muscles. The amount of testosterone released is related to the volume of muscle mass used and the overall intensity of the exercise. Whereas a squat uses the single largest muscle in the body (gluteus maximus) and the largest muscle group (quadriceps), the dumbbell curl uses only the two small muscles of the biceps brachii along with the brachialis and brachioradialis. Clearly the squat is more intense than the dumbbell curl and would be a more effective exercise for releasing testosterone and HGH. Therefore, it can be argued that the squat is a better cue for muscle clocks.

FIGURE 3.1   While high-intensity exercises such as the (a) power squat release adequate amounts of testosterone into the bloodstream to stimulate muscle hypertrophy, small-muscle isolation exercises such as the (b) biceps curl will not.

Human Growth Hormone

Human growth hormone (HGH) is a biochemical, like testosterone, that is critical to muscle growth and strength and power development. Just like testosterone, HGH levels fluctuate naturally. During sleep, 75% of HGH is released (7), with the majority released during the first hour of sleep (7). The fact that HGH is released during sleep emphasizes the critical role of rest to muscle recovery and performance. HGH release during sleep, specifically during the first hour of sleep, is an example of the body's natural rhythms and how they are synchronized to activity–rest cycles during a 24 h period.

Just like testosterone, HGH is released into the bloodstream during exercise. It is common knowledge that compound exercises such as squats and deadlifts, which use multiple joints and large muscle groups, are the most effective in releasing HGH (3). In addition, eccentric contractions (lengthening contractions usually associated with the down phase of a motion) cause more HGH release than concentric contractions (shortening contractions usually associated with the up phase of a motion) (3).

The effects of eccentric contractions on HGH release and resultant muscle hypertrophy are well documented; however, how the speed of contractions affects HGH release is less researched. One study has shown that acute HGH responses and higher concentrations of HGH were seen in resistance-trained men who used a slow-velocity instead of a fast-velocity bench press movement (2). Therefore, both the type of contraction and the speed of contraction contribute to HGH release and to the information skeletal muscle clocks receive about scheduled resistance training.

Muscle Pliability

Muscle pliability changes throughout the day and is a signaling cue to help muscle clocks determine the time of day and anticipate work versus recovery. Muscle pliability is typically greatest between 4 and 6 p.m., indicating that muscles will be most flexible during that time of day. Time of day that a muscle is most pliable is an important time cue for muscle clocks and a factor in muscle performance because muscles generate their greatest force just beyond resting length. A slightly stretched muscle generates the most strength and power.

Eating Habits

No one will deny that the timing of eating relative to any form of exercise is important to muscle performance and recovery. The nutrient makeup of meals and overall caloric intake are critical as well. The exact dietary makeup and caloric intake of pre- and posttraining meals is outside the scope of this book; however, what is relative to timing resistance training and muscle clocks is that scheduled eating can help desynchronize muscle clocks from the master clock (9). In other words, sticking to a regular eating schedule helps skeletal muscle establish autonomy from the master clock.

There is a relationship between regularly scheduled eating and muscle clock expression. However, there is no direct relationship between scheduled eating and a muscle clock phase shift. This is a very important point. Eating is not the primary cue exerting dominance over muscle clocks. Eating alone cannot change the rhythm of muscle clocks and cause a phase shift.

The relationship between scheduled eating and muscle clock activity lies in the fact that skeletal muscle uptakes around 80% of the postprandial glucose load. After a meal, muscle tissue works hard to metabolize glucose in the bloodstream. The relationship between glucose uptake and skeletal muscle activity is an important aspect to how muscle clocks help synchronize skeletal muscles through the entire body. Timed eating and muscle glucose uptake are cues that muscle clocks recognize, helping them determine the time of day and regularly occurring events. Skeletal muscle glucose uptake serves as a cue to multiple body systems and other peripheral tissues, synchronizing them all (10).

Cortisol

Because exercise is a stressor, albeit a positive one, it stimulates the release of cortisol, a stress hormone, into the bloodstream. Cortisol is released in response to emotional stress (such as pain, anger, and fear) and physical work (such as scheduled resistance training). Like most of the body's chemicals, cortisol also has its own natural daily rhythm. Natural cortisol levels are at their highest around 8 a.m. and lowest at 3 to 4 a.m. Similar to other biochemical markers in the body, such as testosterone and HGH, cortisol levels fluctuate throughout the day but also increase or decrease in response to their environment.

The primary function of cortisol is to momentarily suppress unnecessary bodily functions so all resources can go to an immediate threat. For example, cortisol levels surge when someone is running from a predator or escaping a burning building. When a threat is present and cortisol is released, the immune system and reproductive functions are suppressed to help cope with the immediate source of stress. Cortisol release into the bloodstream is supposed to be relatively short lived. However, modern life is full of stress; therefore, cortisol is released constantly.

Consistently high levels of cortisol create a dilemma. Cortisol has been connected to a decrease in skeletal muscle mass. Too much cortisol interferes with amino acid uptake critical to muscle growth. In addition to potentially decreasing muscle mass, cortisol increases free-floating glucose in the body, which ultimately leads to more fat mass. Too much fat combined with less muscle is highly undesirable to performance. Therefore, cortisol levels must be controlled, and scheduled exercise plays an important role in stabilizing levels.

Exercise is a positive source of stress that releases cortisol. One study has shown that when mice were forced to run on a treadmill, serum corticosterone levels increased (14). The fact that corticosterone levels increased during forced running is important because corticosterone levels have been shown to play a role in the exercise-induced phase shift of peripheral clocks (14).

To apply the results of this study to humans, the leap has to be made from corticosterone in rodents to its human counterpart, cortisol. The assumption is that scheduled exercise-released cortisol can help phase-shift muscle clocks in humans. The scheduled release of cortisol would help entrain muscle clocks and teach muscles to activate exercise-related molecular actions at the desired times.

Remember that elevated levels of cortisol for an extended time cause a series of negative effects, such as increased fat mass and decreased muscle mass along with additional health-related problems. Although cortisol increases during exercise, at least one study showed that it decreased on average 24% after 4 weeks of resistance training (1). The overall significance of this finding is important because it shows that resistance training can increase cortisol at scheduled times as a muscle clock entrainment cue and then decrease cortisol over time, leading to improved muscle function and possibly contributing to decreased fat mass, both of which are significant to performance.

Exercise Training and Programming

Finally, and most important to sport and fitness practitioners, are the timing cues that muscle clocks get from exercise training and programming. Remember that muscle clocks use exercise training and programming cues to help regulate muscle performance and synchronize muscles with other body systems. Timing cues are used to reprogram muscle clocks to aid metabolic function related to muscle performance, sleep, recovery, and more (figure 3.2).

Light and other environmental cues entrain the master clock in the suprachiasmatic nucleus (SCN). The SCN then generates internal circadian time cues, such as hormonal, neuronal, and body temperature cycles, to synchronize the peripheral clocks. The musculoskeletal clocks can also be entrained by other time cues, such as food intake and exercise. The circadian rhythms control a variety of genes and pathways crucial for the correct functioning of the musculoskeletal system and entire body. Mutations of the core clock genes can result in disease and impaired function.

The good news is that the timing cues muscles look for are programming variables that all sport and fitness practitioners are familiar with, including mode, frequency, volume, duration, intensity, and rest periods. The only difference is that instead of being strictly programming variables, these same concepts are now viewed as muscle clock entrainment tools as well. The

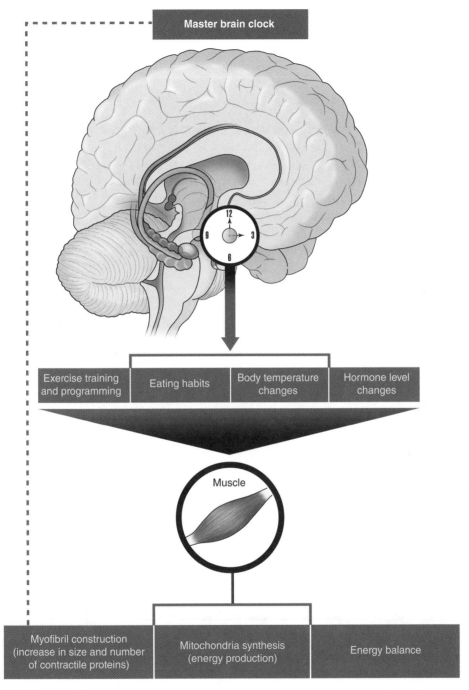

FIGURE 3.2   Effects of timing cues on skeletal muscle via the events associated with muscle contraction, exercise training, and programming indirectly influences the master clock.

Based on Dudek and Meng (2014).

remainder of this chapter is devoted to exercise training and programming cues. Each timing cue is defined and discussed in detail, with suggested programming strategies for how to use cues in workouts and programs featured in part III.

Forced Exercise

The difference between forced versus voluntary exercise is a critical distinction to make when discussing exercise and training cues related to muscle clocks. When examining athletes in research settings, a clear distinction is made between exercise that is forced on someone and voluntary exercise. A good way to think of the difference is that forced exercise is programmed, such as scheduled athletic training sessions in humans and forced wheel running in rats. This is in direct contrast to recreational, by choice, spur-of-the-moment physical activity, such as a pickup basketball game and other spontaneous physical exertion.

Forced exercise changes muscle clock gene expression, causing a phase shift and affecting skeletal muscle performance (15). Scheduled training sessions, although voluntary in terms of participation (no one is actually *forced* to train), help muscle clocks establish a 24 h cycle and have a positive effect on synchronizing muscle clocks to one another and to other body systems, yielding superior training outcomes. Most important, scheduled exercise teaches muscles to anticipate upcoming training sessions and coordinate physiological responses in advance. With scheduled exercise sessions, muscles learn to anticipate activity–rest cycles and click on the molecular mechanisms associated with muscle performance ahead of training.

Clock Entrainment

Regularly scheduled exercise can phase-shift muscle clocks (see figure 3.2). When skeletal muscle contracts, it releases myokines, providing important cues that muscle contraction is occurring. When done on a regular time schedule, the consistent release of myokines signaling skeletal muscle contraction is a cue that entrains the master clock and peripheral clocks.

Scheduled exercise is powerful. It can override the natural light–dark cycle of biological clocks (4, 13, 18). Scheduled training is a cue that helps give muscles autonomy and flexibility in responding to the demands of their unique environment. Scheduled exercise can teach muscles to click on the associated actions of muscle performance at the desired time of day ahead of training, improving the effectiveness of training, reducing the likelihood of interference, and providing muscles with information about when to perform and when to recover.

Session Time of Day

By now is it clear that biological clocks, including muscle clocks, are on 24 h cycles. It is also apparent that all clocks use both external and internal cues to determine the time of day and coordinate tissue-specific actions to specific times and the anticipated activity of local tissues. In the case of muscle clocks, when exercise is scheduled is a critical entrainment cue. Regularly scheduled exercise at a set time of day over the course of weeks and months helps muscle clocks set an internal 24 h rhythm and coordinate skeletal muscle tissue to anticipated resistance training sessions.

Training Frequency

Training frequency is how often exercise is done. Frequency is most commonly reflected as the number of days per week training is performed; however, it can also be the number of sessions within days when more than one training session is done in a 24 h period. Muscle clocks are closely monitoring the frequency and timing of training sessions within each 24 h period to anticipate and set a regular schedule.

As discussed in chapter 2, interference happens when cardiovascular and resistance training are performed too close together in time; however, interference can be avoided by allowing enough time to elapse between the two modes of exercise. Ideally, there should be 4 to 6 h between cardiovascular and resistance training (11), and training sessions should never be within 30 min of one another. To provide consistent cues, cardiovascular training should be performed on alternate days from resistance training (19). Determining a day-to-day training schedule that alternates cardiovascular training with resistance training tells muscles when to be ready to click on the molecular actions associated with cardiovascular versus resistance training outcomes.

Exercise Mode

The mode of exercise is the type of exercise performed. The mode can be as broad as the difference between cardiovascular training such as cycling and resistance training with weights. As discussed in chapter 2, interference occurs when cardiovascular exercise is performed less than 3 h before resistance training. Therefore, making sure that cardiovascular and resistance training are clearly distinguished and separated is important, because the mode of exercise is a cue to muscles to learn when to anticipate cardiovascular or resistance exercise and click on the associated actions with either.

The difference between jogging and weight training is stark; however, mode as a training cue can also be more specific, such as the difference between cycling and running or a jump squat and a back squat. In the squat example, although the biomechanics are similar for the two squats, the plyometric nature of the jump squat changes the mechanics and intensity. These subtle mechanical changes are important because specific patterns of muscle activation are timing cues muscle clocks look for.

The mode or type of exercise, whether cardiovascular or resistance training, is important. As discussed in chapter 2, it is clear that muscles get confused when cardiovascular and resistance training are done within 30 min of each other, let alone in the same session. In terms of exercise training and programming, it is critical to differentiate between cardiovascular and resistance training sessions. For athletics and elite fitness, the programming suggestion is to not combine cardiovascular and resistance training in one session; however, if this cannot be avoided, resistance training must be done first. Each mode provides different cues to muscle clocks, and molecular mechanisms do not have enough time to reset for either mode. As covered in chapter 2, the molecular mechanisms responsible for strength improvements require a minimum of 3 h to reset after cardiovascular training (9).

Cardiovascular, Resistance, and Flexibility Training

Cardiovascular training is defined as continuous aerobic activity, normally ranging from 20 to 60 min of sustained activity. Scheduled cardiovascular training provides muscles with important cues about the time of day and activity–rest cycles. It causes a series of molecular events in muscles specific to cardiovascular endurance training. As mentioned in chapter 2, cardiovascular training should be performed on alternate days from resistance training (19) and for only 20 to 30 min if the training goal is increased strength.

Resistance training is defined as exercise designed to improve muscle mass, strength, and power. Resistance training causes a series of specific molecular events in the muscles being trained. A workout should include 2 to 4 sets of two different biomechanically paired strength exercises. The biomechanical similarity of exercises is the degree to which two movements are alike; it is a critical programming cue, defined later in this chapter and discussed in detail in chapter 4.

Flexibility is defined as the ability of a muscle to relax and yield to stretch. Flexibility exercises lengthen a muscle from its origin to its insertion, stretching a muscle from one end to the other. Muscle pliability is a signaling cue to help muscle clocks determine the time of day and anticipate work versus rest; in addition, muscle pliability is a factor in performance. A muscle lengthened slightly beyond its resting length generates the most force.

The idea that muscles can anticipate is not far-fetched. Muscles are intelligent; they can learn to anticipate and will be ready to perform when provided the right cues consistently, clicking on the associated molecular mechanisms of muscle growth, strength, and power at the same time each day.

Biomechanical Similarity

Because muscle clocks look for biomechanical similarity, the mode or type of exercise is a critical programming cue to entrain muscle clocks. Biomechanical similarity is the degree to which two exercises are similar. In other words, exercise-specific timing cues about the mode of exercise are delivered to muscle clocks based on the type of exercise and the primary joints used and muscles trained. For example, a supine glute bridge is a simple way to use hip extension during an exercise, while a deadlift, a much more complex exercise, also uses hip extension. The point is that each exercise uses hip extension as the primary joint action and thus uses similar muscles; therefore, the exercises are biomechanically similar.

Biomechanical similarity is a training method that pairs two exercises that are alike. Pairing exercises that use similar muscles or muscle groups in similar joint patterns provides muscle clocks with invaluable timing cues. The similarity of movements is an entrainment cue that can help muscle clocks establish a schedule and anticipate upcoming training sessions. With consistent cues using biomechanically similar exercises, muscle clocks learn when to click on the molecular actions associated with resistance training during each 24 h period.

Exercise-specific timing cues are based on the primary joints involved and muscle actions performed. Pairing exercises that use similar joint actions establishes biomechanical similarity, providing an important exercise and training cue. Here is an example of how the biomechanical pairing training method works, using the leg press and back squat exercises.

In the leg press (figure 3.3), the primary muscles trained are the quadriceps, hamstrings, and gluteus maximus. The primary joint actions of the leg press are hip extension and knee extension.

To demonstrate biomechanical similarity, consider the back squat (figure 3.4). In the back squat, the primary muscles trained are the quadriceps, hamstrings, and gluteus maximus, the same as the leg press. The primary joint actions of the back squat are hip extension and knee extension, also the same as the leg press.

A quick comparison of the back squat and leg press shows that they are biomechanically similar. The primary muscles trained and the primary joints involved and muscle actions performed of each exercise match. The biomechanical timing cues between the two exercises are consistent.

Volume

Volume is the amount of exercise done during a training session and can be expressed as the amount of time spent jogging or the distance of a run, for example. In work on concurrent training, as covered in chapter 2, volume is often combined with duration to reflect the total amount of exercise done

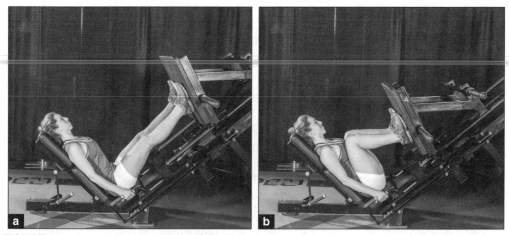

FIGURE 3.3   Leg press: (*a*) start position; (*b*) execution.

FIGURE 3.4   Back squat: (*a*) start position; (*b*) execution.

over a week. Volume is particularly relevant when determining the effects of cardiovascular exercise on resistance training. There is a volume threshold at which cardiovascular training adversely affects resistance training outcomes, and that threshold is 30 min (19).

In terms of resistance training, volume is measured as the number of sets combined with the number of repetitions for each set performed for each exercise and then summed over the session. Although volume itself is not as important to clock entrainment as the frequency and mode of resistance training, it is a critically important factor for peak muscle performance. Combined with the most effective training schedule, finding the perfect balance of sets and repetitions, along with exercise intensity and rest periods, will yield the best outcomes.

Intensity

The intensity of exercise is a measurement of how hard the exerciser is working. It is an indicator of effort. In resistance training, intensity is usually reflected by the amount of external weight or the percentage of a person's maximal effort required to complete one repetition of an exercise. However, body weight and the position of the body relative to gravity also contribute to intensity. For example, a body-weight push-up is made more difficult when the feet are elevated on a bench instead of being on the ground. More weight is displaced on the primary working muscles of the anterior chest when the feet are elevated.

Intensity is also a reflection of the speed of muscle contraction during a resistance exercise (such as a plyometric drill) or the speed of contraction (slow versus fast repetitions). The intensity of exercise is a critical factor for clock entrainment. The higher the intensity of exercise, the more testosterone, cortisol, and HGH are released into the bloodstream. All of these biochemical events are timing cues that contribute to muscle clock entrainment; when released on a regular schedule within 24 h periods, intensity-related biomechanical muscle changes can contribute to phase-shifting of muscle clocks.

Intraset Rest Periods

Intraset rest periods are breaks within resistance training sets. They usually range from 10 to 120 s, and are in direct contrast to traditional rest periods between sets, which can last up to 5 min. The intraset rest training method allows for recovery during the set. Although the allowed recovery is minimal, the intent of an intraset rest period is to provide the athlete with the opportunity to finish the target set and number of repetitions with the original weight instead of reducing the weight or the number of repetitions.

One study set out to determine if resistance training with intraset rest breaks produced greater increases in muscle power compared to traditional rest breaks between sets (12). The researchers examined 22 men ranging in age from 25 to 65 years. Subjects were matched according to their baseline characteristics and assigned to 12 weeks of resistance training using either traditional between-set breaks or intraset rest breaks. Body composition, strength (1RM) on the bench press and squat, power output (using 60% 1RM) on the bench press and squat, and vertical jump were measured before the study began and again after 4, 8, and 12 weeks of resistance training. The results showed that intraset rest breaks produced greater strength gain and power output in the bench press than traditional between set breaks; however, there were no differences reported between groups for squat performance. These findings are important because they indicate that smaller intraset rest intervals are more effective for strength and power improvement than longer between set rests, at least for the upper body.

The findings of this study are exciting to trainers interested in strength and power development, but they are also relevant to muscle clocks and time cues (12). Molecular actions associated with muscle performance are responding to very small time intervals within training sessions that are intensity dependent.

Intensity–Rest Cycles

Another example of timing within training sessions is intensity–rest cycles. The amount of rest required for recovery from one set of an exercise or another varies by the intensity of the exercise, determined by the volume of muscle mass used, the percent of 1RM, and the speed of muscle contraction. For example, based on the time to return to baseline heart rate, a jump squat set requires more rest than an isolation exercise, such as a triceps pushdown. In one study, intraset rest breaks were found to be more effective for strength and power output than longer rests between sets for upper-body exercises only (12). This is a key point because intensity is generally higher for lower-body exercises, and thus the length of rest required to recover is longer than what an intraset break allows. Muscles are monitoring all cues related to exercise mode, frequency, and timing; therefore, intensity–rest cycles give them another cue about what to anticipate when.

Intermittent Rest

Whereas intraset and intensity–rest cycles refer to timing of events during an individual training session, intermittent rest refers to 24 h rest periods between training sessions. The concept of intermittent rest is adapted from the idea of intermittent fasting, which proposes fasting for a certain time and then eating during a certain time. Although there are many variations of intermittent fasting, ranging from hours to days of alternating periods of eating restrictions with free eating, intermittent rest is based on the prescription to fast 2 non-consecutive days per week and eat sensibly on nonfasting days. The general idea behind 2 days per week of intermittent fasting is to stay on the body's natural, traditional 24 h cycle.

The exercise programming suggestion for intermittent rest is the same as intermittent fasting: take 2 nonconsecutive days of rest per week, while training the remaining 5 days per week. An intermittent rest schedule is contrary to the popular 5-days-per-week training with weekends off schedule. The rationale behind an intermittent-rest programming schedule is that the master clock in the brain synchronizes all clocks to a 24 h schedule, and this is reset daily or every 24 h cycle. Therefore, all clocks, including muscle clocks, are looking for 24 h schedules and rhythms. They are monitoring external and internal events to set a schedule and coordinate physiological functions on a 24 h cycle. Taking 72 h off on the weekend or training on Friday morning and not again until Monday morning confuses 24 h clocks.

Specific to exercise training and programming cues, an intermittent-rest schedule provides muscles with valuable timing cues about 24 h phases. Intermittent rest provides muscle clocks with information about the frequency of each mode of training (days per week based on 24 h periods), activity–rest intervals consistent with light–dark cycles, and the time of day, all of which is used to anticipate training each day.

Muscles are intelligent. They can learn to anticipate upcoming training sessions and make the molecular adjustments ahead of time to maximize effectiveness, if they are provided the right consistently timed cues.

Conclusion

Muscle clocks are internal timekeepers monitoring environmental and physiological signals that affect muscles. The muscle clocks learn over time what to expect, when, and how to respond by paying attention to a wide range of cues, including time of day from the master clock in the brain, regularly occurring physiological changes in local muscle tissue, and scheduled exercise programming and training cues. With the right time cues, muscle clocks are able to develop their own 24 h daily rhythms that allow them to anticipate upcoming training sessions and activate in advance the molecular actions associated with muscle performance and recovery, improving resistance training outcomes.

4 | Applying Biomechanical Similarity to Resistance and Plyometric Exercises

Muscle clocks look for *biomechanical similarity*, or the degree to which exercises use the same or similar muscles and primary joint actions. Pairing exercises based on biomechanical similarity provides consistent cues to muscles clocks about what type of exercise to anticipate. To simplify the concept of biomechanical similarity, resistance and plyometric exercises are categorized into six groups: all-body power, bilateral lower body, unilateral lower body, upper body, isolation, and plyometric. Although there are many exercises that can fit into each one of these categories, the exercises featured in this chapter were selected based on

1. the similarity of primary muscles and muscle groups used, and
2. the similarity of primary joint actions.

Biomechanical Similarity

Biomechanical similarity is determined by the similarity of muscle and joint action during two or more exercises within one session. Biomechanical similarity provides cues to muscle clocks that are used to anticipate upcoming scheduled training sessions and to phase-shift internal clocks. Exercise training and programming cues delivered via biomechanical similarity entrain muscle clocks and help them learn when to click on the associated molecular actions with muscle performance.

The degree of biomechanical similarity of paired exercises provides exercise-specific timing cues based on the primary muscles trained and the primary joint actions performed. For example, the triceps pushdown is similar to the overhead triceps extension because both exercises use the triceps brachii muscle and elbow extension as the primary joint action. In a well-planned training program, biomechanically similar exercises that use similar joint actions and muscles are paired together during sessions and on a regular schedule. For example, the pairing of the triceps pushdown and overhead triceps extension is scheduled during sessions at similar times during the day.

When working within the context of biomechanical similarity, it is critical to stay focused on the primary muscles and joints used. For example, a back squat is a common exercise that works many muscles and muscle groups. However, the reason most people include back squats in a workout program is to target the quadriceps femoris and gluteus maximus, not the rectus abdominis, a stabilizing muscle. For that reason, the mechanical analyses of muscles and joints used in exercises examined here focus on the primary muscles and primary joint actions.

Same or Similar Muscles Used

Pairing exercises that use similar muscles with similar primary joint actions provide muscle clocks with cues that help them learn to anticipate upcoming training sessions. With consistent cues delivered using biomechanically similar exercises, muscle clocks learn when to anticipate resistance training during each 24 h period.

A good example of pairing exercises that use the same or similar muscles is to pair the knee extension and back squat. Both exercises use the quadriceps femoris muscles, albeit differently, but the premise holds that the primary muscle group used in both exercises is the quadriceps femoris and the primary joint actions are knee extension and flexion and hip extension and flexion.

Similar Movement Pattern

Biomechanical similarity is also determined by the degree to which two exercises use overall similar motions. For example, a regular push-up and a plyometric push-up are different exercises, but they use the same basic push-up motion. Other examples include a back squat and a jump squat and a Smith machine chest press and plyometric chest press.

Similar Joint Action

Although most people analyze exercises based on which muscles they work, a true biomechanical analysis starts with examining the joint action of an exercise or movement. Pairing exercises that use similar primary joint actions establishes biomechanical similarity. For example, paired exercises can use similar primary joint actions such as shoulder elevation and depression or hip abduction and adduction. In both cases, important exercise and training cues about the type of movements to anticipate are provided to muscle clocks. In the knee extension and back squat example, although one is done standing and weight bearing and the other seated and non–weight bearing, both the squat and leg extension exercises involve extension of the leg at the knee during the concentric phase. Therefore, both exercises are performed using knee extension and flexion, albeit differently, but the premise holds that the primary joint actions are similar.

Active Versus Passive Joint Action

Active joint actions are critical to muscle development and performance as they require muscles to produce force to move the bone around its axis (the joint). An active joint movement can be seen during the upward phase of a biceps curl in which the brachialis muscle must produce force to move the weight up toward the shoulder against gravity.

Contrary to active joint actions, *passive joint actions* are those in which something other than muscle force moves the bone around the joint. Usually this is gravity during the downward phase of a movement. It is important to note that passive joint action also can be caused by someone else, such as a personal trainer or physical therapist inducing the joint movement.

Similar Muscle Activation Patterns

When watching a regular push-up and a plyometric push-up, it is easy to see that the movements look alike, that similar motions and thus muscle activation patterns are used to complete both exercises. Muscle activation patterns are an advanced concept that has its origins in motor unit recruitment theory. Motor units are made up of one motor neuron arriving from the brain that is attached to numerous muscle fibers within a muscle. Motor units are classified as either slow- or fast-twitch fiber specific, and they are recruited in a specific pattern or order—slow twitch to fast twitch—and de-recruited or deactivated in the opposite direction—fast twitch to slow twitch. Exercises that require low force and minimal speed use primarily slow-twitch fibers, and heavy weightlifting exercises and quick movements use slow-twitch fibers to start the movement but rely on fast-twitch fibers for the full execution of the movement.

Whereas motor unit recruitment theory explains how muscle fibers are activated and deactivated, whole muscles are activated differently for similar exercises. For example, different types of squats preferentially activate different target muscles in different ways. In fact, the specificity of muscle activation is determined by very subtle biomechanical changes to an exercise. Muscle activation patterns are so specific that even minor changes in knee placement during a back squat alter the ways primary muscles are used. In one study (2), normal knee placement squats were compared to squats executed with two common form errors: mediolateral (side-to-side) and anteroposterior (front-to-back) knee malalignments. The two knee misalignment squat variations changed muscle activation patterns in the target muscles, specifically increasing activation of the hamstrings and gastrocnemius in a normal, neutral aligned squat. Therefore, when knee placement was changed minimally, it made the squat a less effective quadriceps femoris exercise, showing the effects of mechanics on muscle activation patterns.

To summarize, muscle activation is the order in which slow- and fast-twitch muscle fibers within a muscle are activated during an exercise. Individual muscle fibers will be activated differently for different exercises within a muscle based on the required force and speed of a movement. Muscle activation also describes how individual muscles within a muscle group are activated during an exercise.

Biomechanically similar exercises use similar muscles and primary joint actions. However, subtle alterations in biomechanics and intensity can change which muscles are used and the extent to which fast-twitch fibers are necessary. Hence exercises that look mechanically similar and work the same or similar muscles or muscle groups still can work muscles differently. Because biomechanical similarity is a critical exercise training and programming cue, it is necessary to be aware of subtle biomechanical variations and keep them in mind when designing resistance training programs. It is also important to note that because muscle clocks rely on biomechanical cues it is essential that form errors are avoided and exercises are executed correctly.

Exercise Intensity

As mentioned earlier, the intensity of an exercise determines which types of muscle fibers are used in an exercise. The force required to complete an exercise and its speed determine its intensity, which is reflected by whether or not and the extent to which fast-twitch fibers are recruited.

Muscle force is the output or strength required to complete an exercise while adding speed or velocity to a movement to increase the power. An example of intensity changes is to compare a back squat to a box jump. The intensity of the back squat is determined by the amount of weight lifted; heavier loads focus on developing strength, and moving heavy loads occurs over a slower time. A box jump is a different type of exercise, one characterized by a lack of pause between the rapid *eccentric* (lengthening) action and subsequent *concentric* (shortening) action and by the use of the stretch reflex in muscles to produce power. The intensity of the box jump is determined by how much force can be produced *and* how quickly it can be produced. Force is rarely measured during the box jump. Rather, the height of the box tends to be a surrogate (although sometimes misleading) measure of intensity. The amount of external weight used is less in the box jump than the squat because the movement is quick and the objective is to develop explosiveness instead of strength.

In complex training, for example, a heavy load strength exercise is paired with a biomechanically similar plyometric exercise with the intent to develop both muscle strength and power. Pairing exercises that differ in load and speed but have similar biomechanics varies the work.

Exercise Categories

For the purpose of biomechanical similarity, exercises are divided into six categories: all-body power, bilateral lower body, unilateral lower body, upper body, isolation, and plyometric. In this section, exercises within each category are analyzed based on the muscles used and accompanying primary joint actions. The intent is to analyze the exercises used to build the paired exercise training workouts and programs detailed in chapters 7, 8, and 9.

There are two phases to any resistance training exercise: the eccentric phase and the concentric phase. For the purpose of this book, an analysis of an exercise is limited to the concentric phase and only the corresponding primary joint and muscle actions are described.

The exercise finder (table 4.1) is organized by alphabetical order within each of the six exercise categories (e.g., all-body power, bilateral lower body).

All-Body Power Exercises

Power exercises use many muscle groups at the same time; therefore, they are considered all-body exercises. All-body power exercises are advanced exercises, for suggested use with experienced exercisers only.

For analysis purposes, only the primary muscles and joint actions are included and the movements focus on the concentric phase of the exercises. The reason is to keep the focus on biomechanical similarity. In later chapters, all-body power exercises are paired with other exercises to design workouts and programs for strength and power development. In addition, their use in complex training program design is discussed and demonstrated.

TABLE 4.1 Exercise Finder

Exercise name	Page number
ALL-BODY POWER EXERCISES	
Clean and jerk	71
Hang clean and press	71
Power clean	70
Power shrug	72
Push press	72
Snatch	70
BILATERAL LOWER-BODY EXERCISES	
Back squat	74
Deadlift (traditional)	74
Front squat	73
Leg press	75
Overhead squat	74
Romanian deadlift	75
UNILATERAL LOWER-BODY EXERCISES	
Bulgarian split squat	76
Back lunge	79
Front lunge	78
Side lunge	77
Single-leg squat	79
Step-up	80

Exercise name	Page number
UPPER-BODY EXERCISES	
Bench press	81
Bent-over row	82
Dip	83
Dumbbell fly	82
Push-up	84
Seated row	82
Shoulder press	83
ISOLATION EXERCISES	
Elbow extension	87
Elbow flexion	87
Hip abduction	86
Hip adduction	86
Hip extension	86
Hip flexion	85
Knee extension	85
Knee flexion	85
Neck extension	88
Neck flexion	88
Shoulder abduction	87
Shoulder adduction	87
Shoulder extension	88
Shoulder flexion	88
Shoulder girdle elevation	88

> *continued*

TABLE 4.1 *(continued)*

Exercise name	Page number
PLYOMETRIC EXERCISES	
Bilateral lower-body plyometric exercises	
Box jump	89
Depth jump	91
Depth jump to second box	92
Double-leg tuck jump	91
Jump and reach	90
Squat jump	90
Unilateral lower-body plyometric exercises	
Alternating lateral single-leg pushoff	94
Alternating single-leg pushoff to the front	93
Cycled split jump	96
Jump split squat	95
Lateral double-leg box jump	95
Lateral single-leg pushoff	94
Single-leg pushoff to the front	93
Single-leg tuck jump	97
Vertical jump (single leg)	96

Exercise name	Page number
PLYOMETRIC EXERCISES	
Upper-body plyometric exercises	
Clap push-up	99
Clap push-up (behind the back)	100
Depth push-up	101
Kneeling power ball pass	98
Medicine ball chest pass	98
Medicine ball power drop	100
Plyometric push-up	99
Plyometric Smith machine bench press	100

Snatch

Primary Muscles

- Quadriceps femoris (rectus femoris, vastus medialis, vastus intermedius, and vastus lateralis)
- Gluteus maximus
- Gastrocnemius
- Hamstrings (semimembranosus, semitendinosus, and biceps femoris)
- Trapezius
- Deltoids

Primary Joint Actions

- Knee extension
- Hip extension
- Ankle plantar flexion
- Shoulder flexion
- Shoulder girdle upward rotation and elevation

Power Clean

Primary Muscles

- Quadriceps femoris (rectus femoris, vastus medialis, vastus intermedius, and vastus lateralis)
- Gluteus maximus
- Hamstrings (semimembranosus, semitendinosus, and biceps femoris)
- Gastrocnemius
- Trapezius
- Deltoids

Primary Joint Actions

- Knee extension
- Hip extension
- Ankle plantar flexion
- Shoulder girdle upward rotation and elevation
- Shoulder flexion

Hang Clean and Press

Primary Muscles

- Quadriceps femoris (rectus femoris, vastus medialis, vastus intermedius, and vastus lateralis)
- Gluteus maximus
- Hamstrings (semimembranosus, semitendinosus, and biceps femoris)
- Gastrocnemius
- Trapezius
- Deltoids

Primary Joint Actions

- Knee extension
- Hip extension
- Ankle plantar flexion
- Shoulder girdle upward rotation and elevation
- Shoulder flexion

Clean and Jerk

Primary Muscles

- Quadriceps femoris (rectus femoris, vastus medialis, vastus intermedius, and vastus lateralis)
- Gluteus maximus
- Hamstrings (semimembranosus, semitendinosus, and biceps femoris)
- Gastrocnemius
- Trapezius
- Deltoids

Primary Joint Actions

- Knee extension
- Hip extension
- Ankle plantar flexion
- Shoulder girdle upward rotation and elevation
- Shoulder flexion

Push Press

Primary Muscles

- Quadriceps femoris (rectus femoris, vastus medialis, vastus intermedius, and vastus lateralis)
- Gluteus maximus
- Hamstrings (semimembranosus, semitendinosus, and biceps femoris)
- Gastrocnemius
- Triceps brachii
- Anterior deltoid
- Trapezius

Primary Joint Actions

- Hip extension
- Knee extension
- Ankle plantar flexion
- Elbow extension
- Shoulder flexion
- Shoulder girdle upward rotation and elevation

Power Shrug

Primary Muscles

- Quadriceps femoris (rectus femoris, vastus medialis, vastus intermedius, and vastus lateralis)
- Gluteus maximus
- Hamstrings (semimembranosus, semitendinosus, biceps femoris)
- Trapezius

Primary Joint Actions

- Hip extension
- Knee extension
- Shoulder elevation

Bilateral Lower-Body Exercises

Bilateral exercises can be single-joint or multijoint exercises and include single-muscle exercises, such as knee extensions for the quadriceps femoris, and multiple-muscle exercises, such as squats for the gluteus maximus and quadriceps femoris. For analysis purposes, only the primary muscles and joint actions are included to keep the focus on biomechanical similarity.

Front Squat

Primary Muscles

- Quadriceps femoris (rectus femoris, vastus medialis, vastus intermedius, and vastus lateralis)
- Gluteus maximus
- Hamstrings (semimembranosus, semitendinosus, and biceps femoris)

Primary Joint Actions

- Hip extension
- Knee extension

FRONT SQUAT: (*a*) STARTING POSITION; (*b*) BOTTOM POSITION.

Back Squat

Primary Muscles

- Quadriceps femoris (rectus femoris, vastus medialis, vastus intermedius, and vastus lateralis)
- Gluteus maximus
- Hamstrings (semimembranosus, semitendinosus, and biceps femoris)

Primary Joint Actions

- Hip extension
- Knee extension

Overhead Squat

Primary Muscles

- Quadriceps femoris (rectus femoris, vastus medialis, vastus intermedius, and vastus lateralis)
- Gluteus maximus
- Hamstrings (semimembranosus, semitendinosus, and biceps femoris)

Primary Joint Actions

- Hip extension
- Knee extension

Deadlift (Traditional)

Primary Muscles

- Quadriceps femoris (rectus femoris, vastus medialis, vastus intermedius, and vastus lateralis)
- Gluteus maximus
- Hamstrings (semimembranosus, semitendinosus, and biceps femoris)

Primary Joint Actions

- Hip extension
- Knee extension

Romanian Deadlift

Primary Muscles

- Gluteus maximus
- Hamstrings (semimembranosus, semitendinosus, and biceps femoris)
- Erector spinae

Primary Joint Action

- Hip extension

Leg Press

Primary Muscles

- Quadriceps femoris (rectus femoris, vastus medialis, vastus intermedius, and vastus lateralis)
- Gluteus maximus
- Hamstrings (semimembranosus, semitendinosus, and biceps femoris)

Primary Joint Actions

- Hip extension
- Knee extension

Unilateral Lower-Body Exercises

Unilateral lower-body exercises use only one side of the body to complete the movement, although the opposite side of the body helps support and stabilize the body. Unilateral exercises can use small muscles, like those of the upper arm, but they can also use larger muscles, like those in the thigh. The focus here is on unilateral lower-body exercises that share biomechanical similarity with all-body power exercises.

Bulgarian Split Squat

Primary Muscles

- Quadriceps femoris (rectus femoris, vastus medialis, vastus intermedius, and vastus lateralis)
- Gluteus maximus
- Gluteus medius and gluteus minimus
- Hamstrings (semimembranosus, semitendinosus, and biceps femoris)
- Iliopsoas (minor)

Primary Joint Actions

- Hip extension
- Knee extension
- Hip abduction
- Hip flexion (minor)

BULGARIAN SPLIT SQUAT: (*a*) STARTING POSITION; (*b*) BOTTOM POSITION.

Side Lunge

Primary Muscles

- Gluteus maximus
- Gluteus medius and gluteus minimus
- Quadriceps femoris (rectus femoris, vastus medialis, vastus intermedius, and vastus lateralis)
- Hamstrings (semimembranosus, semitendinosus, and biceps femoris)

Primary Joint Actions

- Knee extension
- Hip extension
- Hip abduction

Front Lunge

Primary Muscles

- Quadriceps femoris (rectus femoris, vastus medialis, vastus intermedius, and vastus lateralis)
- Gluteus maximus
- Hamstrings (semimembranosus, semitendinosus, and biceps femoris)
- Iliopsoas (minor)

Primary Joint Actions

- Knee extension
- Hip extension
- Hip flexion (minor)

FRONT LUNGE: (a) STARTING POSITION; (b) STEPPED-OUT POSITION; (c) LUNGE POSITION.

Back Lunge

Primary Muscles

- Quadriceps femoris (rectus femoris, vastus medialis, vastus intermedius, and vastus lateralis)
- Gluteus maximus
- Hamstrings (semimembranosus, semitendinosus, and biceps femoris)
- Iliopsoas (minor)

Primary Joint Actions

- Knee extension
- Hip extension
- Hip flexion (minor)

Single-Leg Squat

Primary Muscles

- Quadriceps femoris (rectus femoris, vastus medialis, vastus intermedius, and vastus lateralis)
- Gluteus maximus
- Hamstrings (semimembranosus, semitendinosus, and biceps femoris)
- Gluteus medius and gluteus minimus

Primary Joint Actions

- Hip extension
- Knee extension
- Hip abduction

Step-Up

Primary Muscles

- Quadriceps femoris (rectus femoris, vastus medialis, vastus intermedius, and vastus lateralis)
- Gluteus maximus
- Hamstrings (semimembranosus, semitendinosus, and biceps femoris)

Primary Joint Actions

- Knee extension
- Hip extension

STEP-UP: (*a*) STARTING POSITION; (*b*) FOOT ON TOP OF BOX; (*c*) FINISH POSITION.

Upper-Body Exercises

Upper-body exercises use the muscles and joints of the upper body only to complete the exercise, although the lower body and core are used to support and stabilize the body during the movement. Similar to lower-body exercises, only the primary muscles and joints are included in the analysis.

Bench Press

Primary Muscles

- Triceps brachii
- Pectoralis major
- Anterior deltoid
- Serratus anterior

Primary Joint Actions

- Elbow extension
- Shoulder horizontal adduction
- Scapular protraction

BENCH PRESS: (*a*) STARTING POSITION; (*b*) BOTTOM POSITION.

Dumbbell Fly

Primary Muscles

- Pectoralis major
- Anterior deltoid

Primary Joint Action

- Shoulder horizontal adduction

Bent-Over Row

Primary Muscles

- Posterior deltoid
- Latissimus dorsi and teres major
- Trapezius (lower and middle)
- Rhomboids

Primary Joint Actions

- Shoulder horizontal abduction
- Scapular retraction

Seated Row

Primary Muscles

- Posterior deltoid
- Latissimus dorsi and teres major

Primary Joint Actions

- Shoulder horizontal abduction
- Scapular retraction

Shoulder Press

Primary Muscles

- Triceps brachii
- Deltoid
- Trapezius
- Levator scapulae
- Serratus anterior

Primary Joint Actions

- Elbow extension
- Shoulder flexion
- Shoulder girdle upward rotation and elevation

Dip

Primary Muscles

- Triceps brachii
- Pectoralis major
- Anterior deltoid

Primary Joint Actions

- Elbow extension
- Shoulder extension

Push-Up

Primary Muscles

- Triceps brachii
- Pectoralis major
- Anterior deltoid
- Serratus anterior

Primary Joint Actions

- Elbow extension
- Shoulder horizontal adduction
- Scapular protraction

PUSH-UP: (*a*) STARTING POSITION; (*b*) BOTTOM POSITION.

Isolation Exercises

Isolation exercises are single-joint movements. They typically require the use of only one joint at a time and normally focus on one muscle group at a time. Isolation exercises complement compound, multijoint exercises and are used here to build paired workouts focused on biomechanical similarity.

In this section, the exercises are categorized based on the primary joint movement, with common exercises that use that movement listed.

Primary Joint Action: Knee Extension

Primary Muscle

- Quadriceps femoris (rectus femoris, vastus medialis, vastus intermedius, and vastus lateralis)

Common Exercises

Machine seated knee extension and chair knee extension.

Primary Joint Action: Knee Flexion

Primary Muscle

- Hamstrings (semimembranosus, semitendinosus, and biceps femoris)

Common Exercises

Prone (face down) machine knee flexion, seated hamstring curl, and lying hamstring curl with or without bands or external weight.

Primary Joint Action: Hip Flexion

Note: Any hip flexion movement in which the knee is brought toward the torso meets the criteria for hip flexion.

Primary Muscles

- Hip flexors (rectus femoris and iliopsoas)

Common Exercises

Any motion that pulls the knees up and toward the hips (e.g., lying supine single or double straight-leg raise, mountain climber).

Primary Joint Action: Hip Extension

Primary Muscles

- Hip extensors (gluteus maximus, hamstrings [semimembranosus, semitendinosus, and biceps femoris])

Common Exercises

Any motion that pulls the leg back from the hip that is achieved while prone (face down, such as the reverse hyperextension), standing, on all fours (quadruped, such as the bird dog), or supine (such as the glute bridge).

Primary Joint Action: Hip Abduction

Primary Muscles

- Gluteus medius
- Gluteus minimus
- Tensor fascia latae

Common Exercises

Any motion that pulls the leg from the hip to the side of the body that is achieved while lying on one side, standing, on all fours (quadruped), or supine such as machine hip abduction and standing cable lateral (to the side) leg raises.

Primary Joint Action: Hip Adduction

Primary Muscles

- Adductor longus
- Adductor brevis
- Adductor magnus
- Pectineus

Common Exercises

Any motion that pulls the leg back under the hip or toward the middle and across the midline of the body. The motion usually follows hip abduction; however, hip adduction can be performed alone. Hip adduction is most likely done while standing or lying supine (face up). Common examples are machine hip adduction and supine ball squeeze.

Primary Joint Action: Elbow Flexion

Primary Muscles

- Brachialis
- Biceps brachii
- Brachioradialis

Common Exercises

Any variation of the biceps curl.

Primary Joint Action: Elbow Extension

Primary Muscle

- Triceps brachii

Common Exercises

Triceps kickback or overhead triceps extension.

Primary Joint Action: Shoulder Abduction

Primary muscle

- Deltoid

Common Exercises

Lateral dumbbell raise and cable raise.

Primary Joint Action: Shoulder Adduction

Primary Muscles

- Latissimus dorsi
- Infraspinatus and teres minor
- Teres major

Common Exercises

Lat pulldown and pullup.

Primary Joint Action: Shoulder Flexion

Primary Muscles

- Anterior deltoid
- Pectoralis major

Common Exercises

Front dumbbell raise and cable raise.

Primary Joint Action: Shoulder Extension

Primary Muscles

- Latissimus dorsi and teres major
- Posterior deltoid

Common Exercises

Straight-arm lat pulldown and pullover.

Primary Joint Action: Shoulder Girdle Elevation

Primary Muscles

- Upper fibers of the trapezius
- Levator scapulae

Common Exercise

Shoulder shrug.

Primary Joint Action: Neck Flexion

Primary Muscle

- Sternocleidomastoid when both sides of the muscle are working

Common Exercises

Seated machine flexion and harness neck flexion.

Primary Joint Action: Neck Extension

Primary Muscles

- Splenius capitis
- Semispinalis capitis

Common Exercises

Prone or standing neck extension and harness-weighted seated or standing neck extension.

Plyometric Exercises

Plyometric exercises are explosive exercises that include jumps or quick movements that involve the stretch–shortening cycle (i.e., an eccentric action immediately followed by a concentric action). They can be combined with all-body power exercises to design advanced paired complex workouts and programs for power development. For the purposes of this book, plyometric exercises are further classified as bilateral lower-body exercises, unilateral lower-body exercises, and upper-body exercises. The intensity of each exercise is also reflected as low, medium, or high. The intensity of the exercise is determined by the perceived degree of difficulty of the exercise and is classified in accordance with standards by the National Strength and Conditioning Association (1).

Bilateral Lower-Body Plyometric Exercises

Bilateral lower-body exercises use both sides of the body. In the case of plyometric exercises, explosive movements are added to increase the degree of difficulty compared to traditional bilateral lower-body resistance training exercises. Exercise intensity is indicated for each exercise.

Box Jump

Intensity

Low.

Primary Muscles

- Quadriceps femoris (rectus femoris, vastus medialis, vastus intermedius, and vastus lateralis)
- Gluteus maximus
- Hamstrings (semimembranosus, semitendinosus, and biceps femoris)
- Gastrocnemius

Primary Joint Actions

- Hip extension
- Knee extension
- Ankle plantar flexion

Squat Jump

Intensity

Low.

Primary Muscles

- Quadriceps femoris (rectus femoris, vastus medialis, vastus intermedius, and vastus lateralis)
- Gluteus maximus
- Hamstrings (semimembranosus, semitendinosus, and biceps femoris)
- Gastrocnemius

Primary Joint Actions

- Hip extension
- Knee extension
- Ankle plantar flexion

Jump and Reach

Intensity

Low.

Primary Muscles

- Quadriceps femoris (rectus femoris, vastus medialis, vastus intermedius, and vastus lateralis)
- Gluteus maximus
- Hamstrings (semimembranosus, semitendinosus, and biceps femoris)
- Gastrocnemius

Primary Joint Actions

- Hip extension
- Knee extension
- Ankle plantar flexion

Double-Leg Tuck Jump

Intensity

Medium.

Primary Muscles

- Quadriceps femoris (rectus femoris, vastus medialis, vastus intermedius, and vastus lateralis)
- Iliopsoas
- Gluteus maximus
- Hamstrings (semimembranosus, semitendinosus, and biceps femoris)
- Gastrocnemius

Primary Joint Actions

- Hip extension
- Hip flexion
- Knee extension
- Ankle plantar flexion

Depth Jump

Intensity

High.

Primary Muscles

- Quadriceps femoris (rectus femoris, vastus medialis, vastus intermedius, and vastus lateralis)
- Gluteus maximus
- Hamstrings (semimembranosus, semitendinosus, and biceps femoris)
- Gastrocnemius

Primary Joint Actions

- Hip extension
- Knee extension
- Ankle plantar flexion

Depth Jump to Second Box

Intensity

High.

Primary Muscles

- Quadriceps femoris (rectus femoris, vastus medialis, vastus intermedius, and vastus lateralis)
- Gluteus maximus
- Hamstrings (semimembranosus, semitendinosus, and biceps femoris)
- Gastrocnemius

Primary Joint Actions

- Hip extension
- Knee extension
- Ankle plantar flexion

Unilateral Lower-Body Plyometric Exercises

Unilateral exercises work only one side of the body at a time. Similar to bilateral lower-body plyometric exercises, for unilateral lower-body plyometric exercises explosive movements are added to increase the degree of difficulty compared to traditional unilateral lower-body resistance training exercises. Note that exercise intensity is indicated for each exercise.

Single-Leg Pushoff to the Front

Intensity

Low.

Primary Muscles

- Quadriceps femoris (rectus femoris, vastus medialis, vastus intermedius, and vastus lateralis)
- Gluteus maximus
- Hamstrings (semimembranosus, semitendinosus, and biceps femoris)
- Gastrocnemius

Primary Joint Actions

- Knee extension
- Hip extension
- Ankle plantar flexion

Alternating Single-Leg Pushoff to the Front

Intensity

Low.

Primary Muscles

- Quadriceps femoris (rectus femoris, vastus medialis, vastus intermedius, and vastus lateralis)
- Gluteus maximus
- Hamstrings (semimembranosus, semitendinosus, and biceps femoris)
- Gastrocnemius

Primary Joint Actions

- Knee extension
- Hip extension
- Ankle plantar flexion

Lateral Single-Leg Pushoff

Intensity

Low.

Primary Muscles

- Gluteus maximus
- Quadriceps femoris (rectus femoris, vastus medialis, vastus intermedius, and vastus lateralis)
- Hamstrings (semimembranosus, semitendinosus, and biceps femoris)
- Gastrocnemius

Primary Joint Actions

- Knee extension
- Hip extension
- Ankle plantar flexion

Alternating Lateral Single-Leg Pushoff

Intensity

Low.

Primary Muscles

- Gluteus maximus
- Quadriceps femoris (rectus femoris, vastus medialis, vastus intermedius, and vastus lateralis)
- Hamstrings (semimembranosus, semitendinosus, and biceps femoris)
- Gastrocnemius

Primary Joint Actions

- Knee extension
- Hip extension
- Ankle plantar flexion

Lateral Double-Leg Box Jump

Intensity

Medium.

Primary Muscles

- Quadriceps femoris (rectus femoris, vastus medialis, vastus intermedius, and vastus lateralis)
- Gluteus maximus
- Hamstrings (semimembranosus, semitendinosus, and biceps femoris)
- Gastrocnemius

Primary Joint Actions

- Knee extension
- Hip extension
- Ankle plantar flexion

Jump Split Squat

Intensity

Medium.

Primary Muscles

- Quadriceps femoris (rectus femoris, vastus medialis, vastus intermedius, and vastus lateralis)
- Gluteus maximus
- Hamstrings (semimembranosus, semitendinosus, and biceps femoris)
- Gastrocnemius (though more in the trailing leg)

Primary Joint Actions

- Hip extension
- Knee extension

Cycled Split Jump

Intensity

High.

Primary Muscles

- Quadriceps femoris (rectus femoris, vastus medialis, vastus intermedius, and vastus lateralis)
- Iliopsoas
- Hamstrings (semimembranosus, semitendinosus, and biceps femoris)
- Gluteus maximus

Primary Joint Actions

- Hip extension
- Hip flexion
- Knee extension

Vertical Jump (Single Leg)

Intensity

High.

Primary Muscles

- Quadriceps femoris (rectus femoris, vastus medialis, vastus intermedius, and vastus lateralis)
- Gluteus maximus
- Hamstrings (semimembranosus, semitendinosus, and biceps femoris)
- Gastrocnemius

Primary Joint Actions

- Hip extension
- Knee extension
- Ankle plantar flexion

Single-Leg Tuck Jump

Intensity

High.

Primary Muscles

- Quadriceps femoris (rectus femoris, vastus medialis, vastus intermedius, and vastus lateralis)
- Gluteus maximus
- Hamstrings (semimembranosus, semitendinosus, and biceps femoris)
- Gastrocnemius

Primary Joint Actions

- Hip extension
- Knee extension
- Ankle plantar flexion

Upper-Body Plyometric Exercises

Upper-body plyometric exercises are explosive movements that use rapid contraction of the muscles of the upper body to increase strength, power, and speed. Note that the exercise intensity is indicated for each exercise.

Medicine Ball Chest Pass

Intensity

Low.

Primary Muscles

- Pectoralis major
- Anterior deltoid

Primary Joint Action

- Shoulder horizontal adduction

Kneeling Power Ball Pass

Intensity

Low.

Primary Muscles

- Pectoralis major
- Anterior deltoid

Primary Joint Action

- Shoulder horizontal adduction

Plyometric Push-Up

Intensity

Medium.

Primary Muscles

- Triceps brachii
- Pectoralis major
- Anterior deltoid
- Serratus anterior

Primary Joint Actions

- Elbow extension
- Shoulder horizontal adduction
- Scapular retraction

Clap Push-Up

Intensity

Medium.

Primary Muscles

- Triceps brachii
- Pectoralis major
- Anterior deltoid
- Serratus anterior

Primary Joint Actions

- Elbow extension
- Shoulder horizontal adduction
- Scapular retraction

Clap Push-Up (Behind the Back)

Intensity

High.

Primary Muscles

- Triceps brachii
- Pectoralis major
- Anterior deltoid
- Serratus anterior

Primary Joint Actions

- Elbow extension
- Shoulder horizontal adduction
- Shoulder girdle medial glide

Medicine Ball Power Drop

Intensity

High.

Primary Muscles

- Pectoralis major
- Anterior deltoid

Primary Joint Action

- Shoulder horizontal adduction

Plyometric Smith Machine Bench Press

Intensity

High.

Primary Muscles

- Triceps brachii
- Pectoralis major
- Anterior deltoid
- Serratus anterior

Primary Joint Actions

- Elbow extension
- Shoulder horizontal adduction
- Scapular protraction

Depth Push-Up

Intensity

High.

Primary Muscles

- Triceps brachii
- Pectoralis major
- Anterior deltoid
- Serratus anterior

Primary Joint Actions

- Elbow extension
- Shoulder horizontal adduction
- Shoulder girdle adduction

Conclusion

Muscle clocks look for biomechanical similarity. The extent to which two exercises use the same or similar muscles and those muscle groups' primary joint actions determine the biomechanical similarity and provide critical exercise programming and training cues to muscle clocks. Pairing exercises based on biomechanical similarity provides consistent time cues to muscle clocks about what type of exercise to anticipate and when. Knowing which exercise to anticipate and when gives muscles the ability to make molecular adaptations associated with training demands ahead of time and maximizes muscle performance.

PART III | CREATE EFFECTIVE TRAINING PROGRAMS

Part III is a complete guide to using paired exercises to design and implement resistance training sessions. It starts with an exploration of *anticipation training*, which is a concept borrowed from motor learning that highlights muscles' ability to learn to anticipate upcoming training sessions and make the associated physiological changes required for resistance training outcomes in advance of the sessions. Chapter 5 also examines the similarities between neural and muscle anticipation and how muscle clocks use both types of anticipation to improve resistance training outcomes. Within the chapter are programming statements that provide readers with ways to apply the concepts immediately to build resistance training programs.

Chapter 6 builds on chapter 5 and explores the concept of intentional undertraining, proposing the idea that undertraining is a viable training method when the timing of scheduled exercise and activity–rest phases are used as primary programming variables. When a resistance training program focuses on timing and is consistently performed, certain molecular actions occur within muscles and recovery becomes optimized. Intentional undertraining is in direct contrast to resistance training systems focused on volume and intensity alone, which exhaust muscles and often lead to overtraining and underperformance.

The remaining chapters in part III are focused on session and program development. Using the exercises detailed in chapter 4 along with photos of additional selected paired exercises, chapter 7 shows readers how to build single-session workouts and programs using biomechanically similar paired exercises to improve strength. Programming summary statements and many sample routines wrap up the chapter, for immediate application to training.

Whereas chapter 7 focuses on strength outcomes, chapter 8 is a detailed account of how to use biomechanically similar paired exercises to program for power outcomes. Using the complex training method as a guide and select paired photos of the exercises outlined in chapter 4, along with new photos, readers are shown how to build single-session workouts and programs to improve muscle power. The chapter also explores the science behind complex training concepts, such as postactivation potentiation and neural priming, and relates those concepts to the cues that muscle time clocks seek. The chapter also includes programming specifics (such as establishing readiness for plyometric training and proper intensity and volume guidelines) and how to select paired exercises for training methods (for example, agonist–antagonist pairing and other common pairings, such as unilateral–bilateral and upper–lower). Sample routines and programming summary statements wrap up the chapter for immediate use in workouts.

Cardiovascular fitness is paramount to being able to train for strength and power, and it is a required element of any comprehensive sport or fitness training program. Therefore, chapter 9 explores concurrent, multiple mode training sessions and long-term programs. The chapter details how to include cardiovascular exercise in a training program while avoiding interference with muscle size, strength, and power outcomes. Suggested sample routines with specific programming statements wrap up the chapter for immediate application to training.

The final chapter of the book covers how to include flexibility training in a concurrent training program without diminishing muscle strength and power. Muscle pliability is a timing cue for muscle clocks, and it is a stimulus for muscle strength and power. Therefore, it is a critical component of an overall program and cannot be overlooked or left out. Recommendations for designing flexibility programs, with an emphasis on avoiding interference with muscle strength and power performance, are provided, along with ways to approach flexibility as an aspect of recovery.

5 | Training Muscles to Think and Anticipate

Borrowing from motor learning, the field of study that looks at how well-structured training programs influence motor performance, this chapter examines how to use exercise training and programming cues to teach muscles to anticipate upcoming workout sessions. Exercise training and programming methods that teach muscles to anticipate upcoming sessions enhance muscle strength and power outcomes, improving overall muscle performance. The chapter starts by examining what central nervous system and muscle anticipation are and how each relates to muscle clocks, biomechanical exercise pairing, and muscle performance. The chapter also includes discussions on motor learning in aging athletes and how to use biomechanical pairings to improve performance during aging and rehabilitation and concludes with suggested programming and summary statements.

Motor Learning Influences

Motor learning is the process of acquiring a motor skill by which the exerciser, through practice and change, refines and makes the newly learned skill automatic. The goal of motor learning is to solidify the internal central nervous system and motor system processes that lead to a lasting change in an exerciser's capacity for a specific skill. Motor learning, although focused on the study of learning processes, also includes other aspects of performance, such as retention of learned motor skills, hence the relevancy to aging athletes and suggested programming changes later in this chapter. A final aspect of motor learning is skill or exercise transfer, which is taking the lessons learned from mastering one exercise and successfully applying them to learning a similar exercise. The transfer of motor skills is fundamental to the biomechanically paired exercise training method used in this book. Using exercises with similar muscle groups and joint action is beneficial to learning, retention, transfer, and execution of exercises.

Concurrent training and its relationship to interference and muscle performance is particularly relevant to the use of biomechanically paired exercises and, in a more general way, motor learning. As a discipline of study, motor learning helps explain how timing cues are used by muscle clocks. The bottom line is that concurrent training, if not well structured, can be chaotic and cause interference. A well-structured exercise training program provides muscles with clear and concise cues about the timing of exercises and the type of upcoming exercises. In addition, and most relevant to motor learning, exercises must be practiced correctly until they are mastered. Poorly structured practice or incorrectly executed movements do not lead to learning and skill mastery. A biomechanically incorrect or sloppy exercise will not provide the necessary exercise training and programming cues to allow muscles to anticipate. For example, if an all-body power exercise, such as a power clean, is done incorrectly—if the athlete does not fully execute the lower-body part of the motion, for example—the muscles do not receive adequate information about the required leg muscle work or, worse, they internalize the exercise as an upper-body motion only.

Regardless of all other factors, exercise form is critical. Well-structured, correct practice is vital for learning any motor skill, including all resistance training exercises. Structured practice trains both the central and peripheral nervous systems and the muscles to execute the desired movement outcome on demand. Regarding the role of muscle clocks in performance, well-structured programming over time (i.e., *practice*) affords the muscles the luxury to anticipate what is next within each 24 h period. Practice and clean execution of resistance training exercises provide muscle clocks vital time cues. Consistently timed training sessions and programs along with biomechanically paired exercises deliver the most effective cues to muscle clocks, and muscles to learn what type of exercise to anticipate and when during each 24 h period. Timed training also helps muscle clocks do their jobs to improve muscle performance, synchronize the muscles to the other body systems, and improve sleep and recovery.

Central Nervous System Anticipation

In psychology, to *anticipate* something is to be able to predict it and look forward to it happening. Anticipation is a neurocognitive event that involves learning and memory, reward and punishment, and arousal. It requires that the athlete be able to integrate feedback associated with changes in the internal and external state with homeostatic processes and timing mechanisms. Although anticipation can occur within seconds to minutes, motor learning requires longer time frames, such as hours to master a simple new motor skill or months to years to truly master complex motor skills and sequences and know when to anticipate them in exercise training and programming and sport (1).

Biological Cycles

It is well established that humans are on 24 h daily cycles and that all tissue-specific biological clocks are on a 24 h cycle dictated by the master clock in the brain. These predictable circadian rhythms are created using consistent timing cues, like those discussed in part I, which range from the dominant photic (light) and day–night cues in the brain to local tissue-specific timing cues (such as eating habits) in muscle clocks. Based on time cues, athletes learn to anticipate daily environmental events such as the time of day and make a change to local tissues, such as muscles, ahead of those anticipated changes.

Number of Options

For most people, the more choices available, the more difficult it is to make a decision. In motor learning, the more possible movement choices there are, the longer it takes to decide on a response and make it. Reaction time, how quickly a response can occur, is most adversely affected by the number of options available. Reaction time is a nervous system event determined by the time required for the brain to cycle through the possible solutions before initiating a response. The more movement options there are, the longer the neural processing time. When quick responses are required, such as in sports, increased reaction time costs seconds and can mean the difference between winning and losing.

The number of options to choose from to generate a response increases reaction time and negatively affects performance. For example, in soccer, a defender who knows his or her opponent has only two likely moves has an advantage over a defender who must process infinite possibilities before starting a movement.

The number of choices also affects the movement time, the time from starting a movement (reaction time) to completing it. An example of movement time is one repetition in resistance training. Defined as a *discrete movement*, one repetition of any resistance training exercise from a biceps curl to a deadlift has a discernable start and end point. Being able to easily feel when a repetition starts and ends provides muscle clocks with invaluable cues about exercise training and programming. The mechanics of action are clear, and muscles know what to anticipate.

When the number of possible movement choices is limited, movement time is improved. In exercise and training, knowing that a knee extension exercise is the only choice improves the reaction time to start it and the speed of the movement. In contrast, an exerciser who does not know if a squat, deadlift, or lunge is coming next will experience increased reaction and movement times, higher performance anxiety, and ultimately decreased performance.

In motor learning and performance, the number of available movement choices is a critical concept. In relationship to exercise training and programming, consistent cues about which exercises to expect and when reduces the number of options, creating both neural and muscle anticipation and speeding up the reaction and movement times and improving muscle performance.

Uncertainty

Uncertainty is when an athlete does not know what to expect next. Not knowing what to expect and when causes anxiety and slows down reaction and movement times.

In psychology and motor learning, the solution to helping reduce uncertainty is to reduce the number of available choices. In essence, decreasing uncertainty means giving people advanced information about what to expect and when and providing aids to improve performance.

In relationship to exercise training and programming, uncertainty is reduced by pairing biomechanically similar exercises and providing consistent cues about which exercises to expect and when relative to the time of day and the frequency of sessions. Biomechanical similarity and regularly scheduled timing cues create neural and muscle anticipation, speed up reaction and movement time, and enhance performance.

Applications to Sports

In sport and athletic competition, the athlete who can anticipate the opponent's next move has the luxury of advanced information, knowing what to expect on the next play. Advanced information is a distinct competitive advantage in any sport. Anticipatory responses to advanced information are a well-known neural and motor event in sports and training; knowing what to expect and when decreases the time the brain must spend on figuring out what is going on and which movement response to program as a result. What that means to performance is that an athlete can react and move more quickly to counter an opponent's move because the athlete knows what to expect and what to do in response.

During competition and games, opponents constantly provide one another with cues about what to expect next. Athletes who know what to do with that information can anticipate what to do next. They don't have to process a lot of different information, filter through it, and then finally choose a response. Advanced information and the knowledge of what to do with that information give athletes an advantage. This is why studying videos of opponent's play and behavior during competition is a key factor to athletic success. Knowing what to expect in advance reduces the number of possible movement responses, uncertainty, and anxiety and improves performance.

In sports and competition, advanced information includes

- movement sequences,
- posture changes,
- hand gestures,
- eye movements or glances,
- sport-specific play patterns and cues, and
- timing or counting sequences.

Advanced information is a real phenomenon of relevance to today's athletes. In one study, researchers examined how soccer players react to their opponent's body-language cues during games (7). Researchers asked 39 soccer players, ranging in skill from novice to semipro, to lie in a MRI machine, which monitored their brain activity, while watching videos of attacking players coming directly at them. In some clips, the attackers would make sudden movements intended to draw the opposing player out of position, and then the clip would black out. Immediately after the clip blacked out, the players had to choose which direction they would go to stop the ball carrier, based only on the body language they had just seen.

As predicted, experienced players were able to correctly guess the right direction to move significantly more often than were novice players. The brain activity of the experienced players showed that their mirror neuron systems were also active, which happens not only when someone makes an action but also when watching another person execute a skill. In other words, the skilled players were able to correctly anticipate their opponent's actions and initiate an effective response. By watching the attacker coming at them, experienced players were able to anticipate the next movement of their opponent, giving them a competitive advantage.

Advanced information, or the ability to anticipate upcoming events in sports, increases the odds of winning. In exercise training and programming, advanced information, including cues received by using biomechanically similar paired exercises, provides muscles with the ability to anticipate and make local changes ahead of training, which improves the effectiveness of training.

Muscle Anticipation

The brain is much more efficient when it receives advanced information and can anticipate what is next. The same is true for muscles, and, as discussed earlier, the ability of the muscles to anticipate relies on the advanced information the local muscle clocks receive and how they use it to prepare for exercise sessions.

Muscle anticipation is the ability of muscles to use their internal molecular clocks to predict changes in their local environment and make necessary molecular changes associated with exercise training in advance of the session. Just like in sports, when athletes can learn to anticipate their opponent's next move, the same is true for muscles. When muscles learn to anticipate upcoming workout sessions and exercises, they are prepared physiologically for the demands of those exercise and are able to respond quickly to the changes associated with muscle growth, strength, and endurance (figure 5.1).

When muscles know what to anticipate based on the timing cues they receive from scheduled exercise programming along with the types of exercises used during training sessions, they can, through a series of complicated molecular actions, aid muscle performance by

- regulating metabolism,
- reducing body fat,
- building more muscle,
- increasing strength,
- increasing power,
- improving speed,
- improving endurance,
- facilitating better sleep,

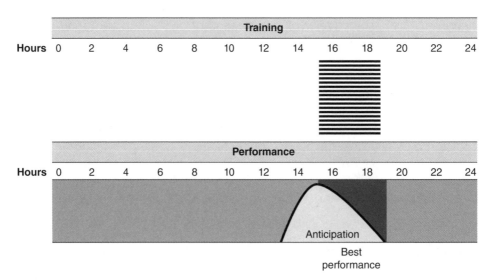

FIGURE 5.1 Muscle anticipation. Using timing cues, muscles learn to anticipate and turn on the molecular actions associated with muscle movement, enhancing performance. Muscles perform best when they can anticipate actions based on cues received from scheduled training sessions and the types of exercises used during those sessions.

Reprinted by permission from A. Mayeuf-Louchart, B. Staels, and H. Duez, "Skeletal Muscle Functions Around the Clock," *Diabetes, Obesity, and Metabolism* 17, suppl. 1 (2015): 39-46.

- fighting fatigue,
- helping prevent metabolic disease, and
- recovering faster.

Biological Cycles

Although 24 h biological cycles are normal and occur with no conscious effort, the ability of muscles to anticipate is a learned skill that occurs over time with well-structured exercise programming and correct practice. However, learning what to anticipate and when begins by paying careful attention to the body's natural, regularly occurring rhythms. Circadian rhythms are the 24 h biological cycles that anticipate daily environmental changes and alter local tissues ahead of those anticipated fluctuations, resulting in long-term adaptations. All internal clocks, including muscle clocks, are on 24 h cycles; therefore, the most effective cues are also delivered around a 24 h cycle. Exercise training and programming cues, such as the type of exercise (cardiovascular endurance versus resistance training) should be scheduled at consistent times each day so muscle clocks can learn to anticipate what type of training will happen when.

Number of Options

As discussed earlier in the chapter, when the number of options to choose from increases, reaction (response) time increases as well. In contrast, when the number of possible choices is limited, reaction time is also reduced. In other words, an athlete who knows what to anticipate and when can react more quickly than one who does not anticipate. The number of options to choose from and then the time it takes to initiate a response or react also affect movement time, or the time it takes to complete a movement once it is started. For example, in resistance training, the movement time is measured from the start of a leg press to its completion. It is the time it takes to make one complete repetition.

In some cases, but not all, a quicker movement time is desired. This would be especially true during power training when the objective is to create muscle force quickly. For example, to develop power, the athlete must perform an exercise such as a depth jump quickly to produce strength as fast as possible over time. Power training uses eccentric muscle contractions and the stretch reflex, which develops quick, explosive movements. Both the mechanics of the depth jump and the type of muscle contraction used are timing cues that muscle clocks use to figure out what type of training is occurring and when. Thus the neural event of knowing what to expect in advance and the muscle being able to anticipate and make local changes ahead of training result in a more efficient response, a quicker move, and enhanced power training.

The effects of the number of choices and complexity of the movement response on reaction and movement have been well documented. In one study, two groups of 24 college-aged men performed two different reaction time tasks (3). One group performed the task using a simple 4 in (10.2 cm) movement from the reaction button to the correct response button; visualize moving the finger from one button on a table to another nearby button. The other group performed a similar task using a complex movement in which they first moved forward 12 in (30.5 cm) to slap a button and then returned to the response button; visualize moving three times farther than the first movement and adding a slap. The second movement is more complex than the first and is the key to the study to determine the differences in movement time between simple and complex movements. Both groups performed 20 trials under each choice condition (the first, simple movement versus the second, more complex movement).

Although these are rather simple movements and not necessarily reflective of resistance training exercises, the results showed that for the complex movement task, the one choice reaction time was significantly faster than the multiple-choice reaction time; when the participants knew in advance that they were going to have to do the complex movement, they were better at it. In the end, what the study showed was that when the upcoming movement is complex and as the number of choices increases, the movement time increases; therefore, the number of movement options increases the movement time for complex motions such as those associated with compound strength training.

The results of the study suggest that when exercisers know which exercises to anticipate in advance and have fewer exercise choices, they can start the movement more quickly and execute it faster, supporting the idea that muscles are able to anticipate and the value of using biomechanically similar paired exercises (3). Well-timed exercise training and programming and paired exercises mean less time spent making a decision about which exercise to do and increased reaction and movement times. In other words, advanced information allows the exerciser to focus on the exercises being performed instead of trying to figure out what is next and then programming a response.

Applications to Resistance Training Outcomes

The central and peripheral nervous systems perform better with the help of advanced information, or knowing what movement to expect in advance. Movement performance is also affected by the number of options available and the complexity of movement. What that means to resistance training programming is that the fewer choices available and the less complicated the exercises are, the better muscle performance will be. Pairing biomechanically similar movements keeps exercise sessions focused on using similar muscle groups and joint actions, while decreasing movement options and movement complexity to aid muscle performance.

Programming

Strategically designed and executed exercise training and programming methods can teach muscles to anticipate upcoming sessions, make the local physiological changes in advance, and improve muscle performance. Anticipation can occur within minutes to years, and in the case of resistance training and programming, muscles need weeks to months to learn a regular schedule and to anticipate upcoming exercises.

When most exercise professionals think of long-term programming, periodization training comes to mind. Periodization training is relevant to both muscle performance and anticipation and occurs over a typical calendar year. As mentioned earlier, motor learning for complex motor skills is not immediate and requires a well-structured and correct practice that can last up to years.

Duration

The process of learning correct resistance training exercise mechanics and providing the body with the time to make the long-term physiological adaptations associated with training takes time. A true periodization training program is built around a typical calendar year, with each cycle lasting weeks to months. Although most people will not design and implement a full 12-month exercise program, periodization cycles are a valuable way to think about the relationship among resistance training timing, muscle clocks, timing cues, and anticipation in both the long and the short term.

Biomechanical Pairings

By now it is clear that biomechanical similarity is a training method that pairs two exercises that are alike, that use similar muscles and muscle groups and joint actions. By pairing similar exercises at consistent time intervals within a 24 h period, those muscle contractions and joint movements are consistent entrainment cues that help muscle clocks establish a schedule and anticipate upcoming training sessions, learning when to click on the molecular actions associated with resistance training during each 24 h period.

Relationship Between Volume and Intensity

Volume is the amount of exercise done during a training session. In resistance training, the volume is the total number of repetitions and sets completed for each individual workout. The volume might also be combined with the frequency (days per week) of training to reflect the total amount of work done over a week.

Whereas volume is how much work is done, the intensity is how hard the exercise is. In resistance training, the intensity is represented by a percent of an exerciser's one repetition maximum effort. The maximum effort may be measured accurately or estimated. Either way, the important thing to remember is that the intensity of effort reflects the difficulty of an exercise, whether it be the amount of weight lifted or the speed on a treadmill.

Typically, the volume of work done is proportionate to how hard the exercise is. In other words, there is an inverse relationship between volume and intensity of exercise, and that is important to muscle anticipation. From what is known about muscle clocks and muscle performance, it appears that muscles not only recognize timing cues, such as the time of day that an exercise will be done, but also learn to anticipate the intensity, making local tissue adjustments ahead of time to reflect anticipation of high-intensity exercise (6).

The ability of muscles to anticipate the intensity of exercise is paramount to programming success. What it shows is that muscles recognize the difference between not only modes of exercise, such as cardiovascular endurance and resistance training, but also modes of resistance training, such as strength versus power training. Training for strength and power outcomes look different, are executed differently, and appear to be recognized as different by muscle clocks. Intensity, or amount of weight lifted, is typically higher with resistance training focused on muscle strength outcomes; resistance training for power outcomes often uses a lower weight to produce more rapid muscle contractions. The intensity, the intended outcomes, and the muscle action is different for the two modes of resistance training, and muscle clocks appear to notice these differences and make local muscle adjustments in anticipation. Although chronic long-term adaptations associated with training will not occur after one workout, the effectiveness of a single-session workout can be improved significantly by using biomechanically paired exercises. And just as confusion occurs between competing modes of exercise, nonfocused chaotic resistance training will yield poor results. Performing exercises that use similar muscles and muscle groups and joint actions during a single workout session targets specific muscles and movement patterns, leading to improved performance.

Scheduled Rest and Recovery

Scheduled rest is essential to exercise programming because it helps provide timing cues to muscle clocks about when to expect rest and engage in active recovery. Scheduling cues muscles as to when to make the local tissue adjustments in anticipation of training or rest because the mechanisms associated with training are different from those associated with recovery.

Scheduling rest periods also prevents overtraining. If there is too little rest, muscles do not adequately repair after a workout session, and muscles cannot undergo the processes of growth. In that case, performance results are minimal, and injury can result. However, if there is too much rest, detraining can occur. Scheduled rest requires a balance between enough rest to build versus too much rest that undermines muscle growth.

It is essential to muscle performance to provide muscles with adequate rest while avoiding detraining. It is also critical to distinguish between rest and recovery, and both are paramount to effective exercise programming. Rest is what people do after training and is a piece of the overall scheduling puzzle. Recovery is a series of active physiological processes that occur both during sessions and after workouts. Recovery processes ensure the associated positive muscle changes that improve muscle performance.

Recovery is active. During exercise, active recovery is something like jogging in place or dynamic stretching between resistance training sets. Although, during resistance training workouts, between-set recovery periods are more recognized, within-set recovery periods are also important. Minimal recovery can occur within sets and is most often used with high-intensity resistance training programs and advanced exercisers. At least one study has shown that small intraset recovery periods ranging from 10 to 120 s produced greater strength and power output in the bench press than traditional longer between-set rest breaks (4). The most likely reason is that muscles are given a short rest and then must work harder to complete a set without full recovery, forcing them to use more muscle fibers within a muscle.

Scheduled rest, both within sessions and between, is a vital part of the exercise programming equation. Rest provides time for recovery, and it is a huge part of entraining muscle clocks on a 24 h cycle. Scheduled rest uses timing cues to teach muscles when to anticipate work versus recovery.

Sample Program

Table 5.1 shows how to structure weekly exercise training to benefit from muscles' ability to anticipate.

TABLE 5.1   Anticipation Programming

Day	Time	Resistance training exercise	Exercise intensity	Volume (sets × repetitions)
Monday	4 p.m.	Back squat	65%-85% 1RM	3-5 × 6-10
Tuesday	Rest			
Wednesday	4 p.m.	Back squat	65%-85% 1RM	3-5 × 6-10
Thursday	4 p.m.	Other resistance training	Other resistance training	3-5 × 6-10
Friday	4 p.m.	Back squat	65%-85% 1RM	3-5 × 6-10
Saturday	Rest			
Sunday	4 p.m.	Back squat	65% 85% 1RM	3-5 × 6-10

Programming Summary Statements

To best use both the brain's and the muscles' ability to anticipate in programming, remember the following key points.

- Uncertainty causes anxiety and decreases the performance of most tasks, including motor tasks.
- In exercise training and programming, the ability to anticipate improves muscle performance by speeding up both reaction and movement times.
- Muscles can learn to anticipate upcoming training sessions; therefore, a regular exercise schedule is critical.
- Scheduled training sessions teach muscles when to click on the molecular actions associated with muscle endurance or muscle hypertrophy, strength, and power.

Age-Related Decline in Anticipation

Any discussion of motor learning must include aging because aging is associated with a marked decline in the ability to anticipate upcoming motor events (5). Anticipatory motor planning abilities develop and mature as children grow older, continue to develop throughout childhood, and likely are stable throughout the lifespan. However, by the seventh decade of life, motor planning performance dramatically declines, with anticipatory motor planning abilities falling to levels of those shown by children.

At present, the processes enabling successful anticipatory motor planning in general and the cognitive processes mediating age-related changes remain unknown. Thus, the aims of a study by Stöckel et al. (5) were to identify the cognitive and motor functions most affected by normal aging and determine the key cognitive and motor factors critical to successful motor planning and muscle performance. Two groups of participants were used: a young group (average age 23 years) and an older adult group (average age 73.5 years). As expected, the test results indicated that normal aging was associated with a marked decline in all aspects of cognitive and motor functioning. Age-related declines were more apparent for fine motor skills, such as those associated with finger pinching. As expected, the neural processing speed and cognitive flexibility (the ability to quickly shift from one idea to the next) was also shown to be adversely affected by age.

Up to 64% of the variability in motor planning performance across age groups could be explained by the cognitive functions processing speed, response planning, and cognitive flexibility, indicating that age-related motor deficits can largely be explained by neural events. Therefore, it is reasonable to suggest that anticipatory motor planning abilities are strongly influenced by cognitive control processes, which seem to be key mechanisms to compensate for age-related decline.

These findings are important to programming effective workouts for aging athletes and support the use of a biomechanically paired training method. The findings back up the general idea that neural anticipation affects muscle performance and that cognitive motor processes steadily decline with age, suggesting that simpler and more focused training methods, such as biomechanical pairing, are more appropriate than others for aging athletes.

The reason is that with the biomechanically paired method the exercises are similar, and thus there is less for the central nervous system to process. Similar movements focusing on the same muscle groups and joint actions requires less cognitive flexibility; athletes don't have to shift between two or more ideas (or movements) as quickly. Biomechanical pairing also facilitates the transfer of motor skills, the ability to learn one movement and transfer it easily to the acquisition of a similar movement. In exercise training and programming, the transfer is critical. For example, once a wall squat is learned correctly, that motor skill can be easily transferred to any number of other similar exercises, such as a front squat or back squat, and later into more complex squat variations, such as split squats.

Conclusion

Motor learning is a historical discipline of study founded in neuroscience; however, the idea that muscles can use their internal clocks to anticipate relies on thinking about motor learning and muscles together in a new way. The key is to acknowledge that muscles are not simple effectors under central nervous system control. Muscles have been shown to have the ability to anticipate and initiate action independently. Using their molecular clocks for guidance, muscles can learn to anticipate scheduled exercise training and programs. That means with a regular routine or schedule, muscles anticipate training and actually prep themselves for results in advance. Muscle clocks learn when to click into action based on the cue or cues they receive to help build muscle, increase strength, improve speed and endurance, and aid in recovery processes. Muscles are independent biological systems with their own natural rhythms and local processes that, once understood and tapped into, can take strength and conditioning training to the next level and into the future.

6 | **Undertraining to Maximize Performance**

The concept of intentional undertraining is not new and has been explored in relation to managing training loads; however, the exploration of how muscle clocks and the strategic timing of resistance training fits into a program that includes intentional undertraining is a contemporary way to examine undertraining and is the focus of this chapter. In this chapter, it is proposed that intentional undertraining is a viable training method when using timing cues (such as scheduled exercise training and activity–rest phases) as primary exercise programming variables. The assumption is that when a resistance training program that focuses on timing is consistently performed, muscle clocks deliver exercise training and programming cues that trigger molecular actions in advance of workout sessions to increase muscle performance and improve outcomes.

Intentional undertraining is in direct contrast to training systems that focus on increasing training volume and intensity alone, which can exhaust muscles and lead to overtraining. In comparison, intentional undertraining is in alignment with exercise programming strategies that focus on monitoring training load in relationship to the timing cues delivered to muscle clocks and the body's responses to those cues. In the last part of the chapter, differential training methods are explored that show how to vary exercise training and programming to build workouts and sessions.

Training Load

Training load is the cumulative effect of training frequency, volume, and intensity. If two athletes each train a total of 350 h per year but have different training intensities over those hours, then the training load is different. In addition to looking at training load over a total year, the training loads of each session and week are also carefully monitored and taken into account to avoid overtraining and optimize performance outcomes.

External Training Load

External training loads measure the amount of work done during training and as part of competitive events. They are quantified by analyzing common programming variables, such as training mode (all-body power exercises versus plyometric exercises, for example), frequency, number of sets and repetitions, and intensity. External training loads are indicators of muscle performance factors (such as strength, power, speed, and acceleration) and are measured by specific tests of muscle capacity.

Internal Training Load

Whereas external training load can be viewed as what the body is subjected to during training, internal training loads reflect how the body responds to the external loads and can be described as the physiological and psychological stressors that occur during training or competition. Common ways to measure internal training loads and the body's response to the total training load include heart rate, blood lactate levels, oxygen consumption, and rate of perceived exertion.

Training Load Integration

External and internal training loads work together. Although they reflect different aspects of training and are defined and measured separately, they are interdependent. For example, it is not uncommon for an athlete to train at a similar external training load (in which the volume and intensity of resistance training are similar) during two consecutive or nonconsecutive training sessions, but then have two different internal training load responses when heart rate and rate of perceived exertion are measured. The inconsistency between external and internal training loads reflects the fact that the body's responses to training loads vary across days and are due to any number of factors, such as fatigue, sleep quality, other personal stressors, and recent training history.

Fatigue Markers

Fatigue markers are a way to quantify tiredness in athletes and to recognize common signs of overtraining, so training loads can be modified. The presence of fatigue markers is associated with an increased risk of injury and illness during and after training and competition and thus underperformance. Fatigue markers include physiological factors such as muscle activity as measured by electromyograpy (EMG), which measures the strength and frequency of electrical activity, muscle deoxygenation, oxygen uptake, and heart rate and psychological factors such as perceived quality of sleep and rest measured by the Recovery–Stress Questionnaire (RESTQ). When all factors are taken into account, the physiological and psychological fatigue indicators reflect the overall well-being of the athlete and the likelihood of overtraining and underperformance.

All fatigue markers are important; however, sleep quality is probably the most important determinant of muscle recovery, psychological well-being, and performance during training and competition. Sleep deprivation negatively affects perceived well-being and adversely affects muscle performance and the quality of training sessions. Poor sleep quality is a huge issue among athletes and anyone who regularly does high-intensity exercise. One review study showed that when more than 1,600 studies were analyzed to determine the quality of sleep among athletes, athletes were shown to take longer to fall asleep, wake up more, report nonrestorative sleep, and have excessive daytime fatigue, all adversely affecting training quality and muscle performance (5).

Training Ratios

Although fatigue is not entirely avoidable it can be decreased if the mode, frequency, volume, and intensity of training sessions are carefully monitored and strategically manipulated over time. Training ratios reflect the relationship between the acute (one bout) to chronic (over time) workload ratio. Training ratios are broken down into two categories: weekly acute training load and chronic training load over weeks or months.

Both acute and chronic training loads are important. Acute training reflects the mode and total volume and intensity of training of one workout session, whereas chronic load is the total training load as reflected by mode, frequency, volume, and intensity of training over time. When considering the role of exercise training and programming as a timing cue to muscle clocks and the role of biomechanical pairing of exercises during sessions, it is easy to see how selecting the correct exercises (mode) and carefully monitoring all aspects of frequency, volume, and intensity over time can deliver consistent timing cues to muscles, enhancing muscle performance.

Intentional Undertraining

Overtraining is counterproductive, and it can even be deadly. Overtraining disturbs the body's natural cycles and rhythms and causes desynchronization of biological systems. In addition to disruptions that are easy to see, overtraining also increases free radicals, which are unstable atoms that cause negative changes to protein cells inside muscles and oxidative damage and can lead to disease (8).

Overtraining also leads to unwanted catabolism, or muscle breakdown. And to make matters worse, training too much causes the body to produce cortisol, a stress hormone that causes more muscle breakdown and the body to retain fat mass.

Undertraining is a possible solution to the threats of overtraining and to help modulate training loads. However, the problem is that most people tend to think that undertraining means underperforming. This line of thought has led to overdoing both training volume and intensity, which can lead to overtraining, fatigue, and injury—all of which can cause poor performance during workout sessions and competition and even cause injury and death.

One way of thinking about the efficacy of undertraining is to reflect on the fact that sports are complex, and, as discussed earlier, fatigue and other personal factors such as alertness, stress, and mental state affect session training outcomes even if training load is the same. Simplified exercise programming, such as using biomechanically similar exercises and consistent programming time cues, uses muscle clocks and is a way to prepare muscles for training and competition while avoiding overtraining from movement paradigms and increasing volume and intensity only.

Resistance training does not need to be complex to be effective, in either exercise selection or programming, and the data on muscle clocks support that claim. As suggested in earlier chapters, exercise selection can come down to easily pairing biomechanically similar exercises that provide muscle clocks with critical exercise training and programming cues, while regularly scheduled exercise and carefully programmed training loads can help muscle clocks learn what to anticipate when and click on adaptations associated with muscle performance even before training begins.

What is done during training sessions is an important part of the overtraining equation, but recovery is equally important to get the desired muscle performance outcomes. In exercise training and programming, rest is as important to training outcomes as the training load itself. It is imperative to keep in mind that intensity or volume can be increased at will to meet a specific performance goal, but overcoming overuse injuries and the variety of physiological and psychological effects of overtraining are much more complex; therefore, approaching training with the mind-set that muscles are intelligent and can learn to aid in training outcomes is paramount.

New Approach to Muscle IQ

The discovery of muscle clocks shows that muscles are autonomous and can act intelligently. With the right exercise training and programming cues, muscles can learn to anticipate and know when to click on the molecular actions associated with muscle performance. The notion that muscles are simple effectors under central nervous system control without autonomy or any regulatory role no longer holds up. Muscles are both intelligent and autonomous, and this idea is supported by the presence of independent muscle clocks inside each of the over 600 skeletal muscles. Muscle clocks are made up of many unique genes that receive timing cues from their external and internal environments and then express themselves in a way that facilitates muscle performance. The fact that muscle clocks demonstrate differential gene expression at different times during the day and in response to different timing cues shows that muscles are intelligent, can respond to their environment, including changes caused by exercise training and programming, and are autonomous regulators within the human body, not effectors only.

Muscles Are Not Beasts of Burden

Muscles are not beasts of burden, nor are they simple effectors under central nervous system control. Muscles make up more than 40% of the body's total mass, and the discovery of muscle clocks has shown that they are independent biological systems with their own inner time clocks, natural rhythms, and local tissue processes that both respond to the environment and other body systems and play a role in regulating the entire body's functioning. Taking into consideration muscles' unique ability to anticipate and self-govern, trainers and coaches have a new and intelligent way to approach resistance training that moves beyond just increasing volume and intensity of training, which leads to overtraining.

Muscles Can Anticipate

The brain is much more efficient when it receives advanced information and can anticipate what is next. Muscles are the same way, and, as discussed in chapter 5, the ability of muscles to anticipate relies on the information local muscle clocks receive about exercise training and programming and how they use that information to prepare for upcoming training sessions.

Muscle anticipation is the ability of muscles, using their internal molecular clocks, to anticipate changes inside and outside their local environment and make the associated molecular changes associated with resistance training in advance. As in sports, where athletes can learn to anticipate their opponent's next move with the right training and information, the same is true for muscles. When muscles learn to anticipate when upcoming workout sessions occur and what exercises might be included, they are able to prepare physiologically for the demands of exercise and are able to respond quickly to the changes associated with muscle growth, strength, and power.

Although 24 h biological cycles are normal and occur with no conscious effort from the brain or local tissues such as muscles, the ability of muscles to anticipate is a learned skill that occurs over time with a well-structured exercise program. Learning what to anticipate and when begins with paying careful attention to the exercise training and programming cues provided and making the changes to local tissues ahead of those anticipated changes. The ability of muscles to anticipate upcoming workout sessions results in the positive long-term adaptations to chronic exercise.

All internal clocks, including muscle clocks, are on 24 h cycles; therefore, the most effective cues are delivered around a 24 h cycle as well. Exercise training and programming cues, such as the type of exercise (cardiovascular endurance versus resistance training) and the mode (biomechanically paired exercises), should be scheduled at consistent times each day so that muscle clocks can learn to anticipate what type of training will happen when during each 24 h period.

Muscles Can Communicate

The idea that skeletal muscle influences other tissues is no longer novel. It is clear that muscles use muscle clocks and the release of myokines in response to muscle contraction as a way to crosstalk and network with one another and other tissues and systems. When muscles release myokines into the bloodstream, they are relaying to the body that muscle contraction is occurring. Other clocks, such as the master clock in the brain, recognize the signals that myokines send, knowing that at that time of day muscles are contracting and activity, not rest, is occurring. In addition to resetting clocks, it is also evident that skeletal muscle contraction leads to changes in the body, such as stimulating glucose uptake, that aid muscle performance and recovery.

It is recognized that muscles communicate with other tissues and organs via the release of myokines. As noted, when skeletal muscle contracts, myokines are released into the bloodstream and travel to other tissues, relaying information about the timing and type of muscle activity. This information is critical to helping the body's internal clocks establish activity–rest patterns and day–night cycles. Also known as crosstalk, communication among tissues via myokines facilitates synchrony with other tissues, maintaining alignment between circadian cycles across tissues. Disrupted or asynchronous skeletal muscle rhythms affect the entire body.

The fact that networking and crosstalk occur and that information is relayed to other body systems about when muscles contract is a critical point to the premise of this book. It highlights the value of scheduled exercise, consistency in the mode of exercise, the autonomy of muscle, and the wisdom of using these unique features of muscles intelligently to aid in developing effective resistance training programs that rely more on timing cues and less on only increases in volume and intensity.

Provide Muscles With Timing Cues

The timing cues that muscle clocks get from exercise training and programming are the most important aspect to understanding the value of muscle clocks to resistance training programming, how exercise affects other body systems and clocks, and how intentional undertraining works. What is important to remember is that muscle clocks use exercise training and programming timing cues to help do their job of regulating muscle performance and synchronizing muscles with other body systems. Local muscle performance and total body synchronization aids in optimal sport and fitness performance and recovery. With strategic timing cues, even those associated with low- to moderate-intensity training, muscle contractions are used to reprogram muscle clocks to aid in processes such as metabolic function related to muscle performance, anticipation, and recovery.

Avoid the Volume and Intensity Trap

Increasing training volume and intensity alone exhausts muscles and leads to overtraining. Although training load is defined as the cumulative effect of training volume and intensity, it is critical to not fall into the trap of increasing and decreasing volume and intensity only. A more intelligent approach is to use simplified exercise programming tools (such as biomechanically similar exercise) and training methods (such as compound, complex, and contrast training methods, discussed in later chapters) and consistent programming timing cues. These approaches help entrain muscle clocks to prepare muscles in advance for training and competition, which will prime them for optimal performance and outcomes while avoiding overtraining from increasing volume and intensity.

Rationales for Undertraining

Overtraining is a result of training too frequently or of increasing training volume and intensity too much. Overtraining is characterized by fatigue, depression, loss of motivation, anxiety, inability to concentrate, increased blood pressure, increased heart rate, increased rate of injury, chronic muscle soreness, delayed recovery, poor sleep, and insomnia (7), all of which are detrimental to muscle performance.

It is clear that overtraining does not lead to optimal muscle performance. However, it is tough to determine ideal training loads given that personal factors, such as sleep quality, have a significant effect on how external training loads influence internal training loads and muscle performance outcomes. The unique relationship between high-intensity training loads and sleep disturbances further highlights the rationale for intentional undertraining. Training can be ineffective, regardless of training load, if the athlete is tired and not feeling well. Thus, intentional undertraining can be a viable solution to help mitigate the relationship between high-intensity exercise and sleep disturbances. Although it is not suggested that all workouts be of low to moderate intensity, periodic intentional undertraining, when strategically used, is a solution to sleep disturbances and their long-term effect on training efficacy and muscle performance. Because intentional undertraining is a training method that relies on muscles' ability to recognize timing cues, it can be used to improve the efficacy of periodic low to moderate training.

Neural Fatigue

Neuromotor fatigue occurs when the brain gets tired and loses its ability to effectively send signals to the muscles and cause contractions. Loss of neuromotor ability, or the ability of a nerve to generate a sustained signal to muscles, is a serious threat to training for positive muscle outcomes. Like any fatigue, neuromotor fatigue can be dangerous because it can lead to submaximal muscle contractions, reduced amounts of force production, poor exercise mechanics, muscle failure, and injury.

Muscle Fatigue

Muscle fatigue occurs when a muscle can no longer generate force. Muscle fatigue is caused by either neural fatigue or the reduced ability of the muscle fiber to contract. When a muscle cannot contract well, the most likely cause is metabolic fatigue, which occurs when muscle work has exceeded the rate of ATP production.

Muscle fatigue can be triggered by changes in muscle contractility caused by too much high-volume and high-intensity training coupled with too little recovery time. Muscle fatigue is a natural part of training and not always a negative event when it is not accompanied by overreaching and overtraining. Too much muscle fatigue leads to poor performance; thus optimal recovery times are paramount and indicate how intentional undertraining might be used to minimize fatigue and optimize training outcomes.

Muscles lose the ability to contract and can fatigue rapidly under high-intensity and high-volume training conditions. This is a rationale for considering alternative training methods that do not rely only on increasing intensity and volume. Pairing biomechanically similar exercises has been explored throughout this book as a viable training method; the simplicity offers reliable and predictable timing cues to muscle clocks and aids performance. Here, pairing biomechanically similar exercises is asserted as a tool that helps manage training loads.

As discussed later in this chapter, contrast resistance training is a method that uses low-intensity training in lieu of moderate- to high-intensity training in combination with high-intensity training. Like complex resistance training discussed in chapter 8, the contrast training method exploits the value of the low-intensity exercise using postactivation potentiation, a neural event that prepares the nerves for quicker action and to better recruit the desired muscle fibers faster. Postactivation potentiation asserts that a similar exercise done before another exercise will make the muscle fibers more responsive for the second exercise. Therefore, the pairing of similar exercises of low and high intensity is a way to increase training loads and efficacy without increasing intensity only.

Benefits of Undertraining

Overtraining is characterized by a number of negative outcomes, as listed earlier in the chapter (7), which are detrimental to muscle performance. Contrary to overtraining, intentional undertraining should not result in over-tiredness, sleep disturbances, and the other symptoms of overtraining, which can render workouts and training programs ineffective. Some of the benefits of undertraining are reduced risk of injury or death due to acute fatigue, improved muscle performance, and enhanced recovery including improved sleep quality.

Reduced Risks of Injury or Death

Overtraining is counterproductive and destroys the body's natural cycles and rhythms. Overtraining can result in muscle performance decrements, periods of detraining, and real competition losses. In competition settings, contact sports in particular, overtraining can be deadly. The effects of fatigue plus decreased mental alertness and the inability to concentrate can be cata-strophic in contact sports in which a keen sense of the opponent's actions and the ability to respond properly are critical for avoiding injury or worse.

The realities of overtraining can be thought of this way: Too much offense in the form of exercise training and preparation breaks down the body's natural defenses, leading to self-destruction of the body's tissues, which can result in disease. Overtraining increases free radicals, which damage tissues. Free radicals are produced naturally, but under normal circumstances, they are broken down and removed by the body. However, in excess, they can lead to oxidative damage to muscles.

Reduced Risks of Overtraining Syndrome

Because intentional undertraining uses low-intensity exercises and reduced training frequency along with increased periods of rest, it reduces the risk of overtraining. When intentional undertraining is programmed into long-term programs and used strategically within sessions, it helps prevent the risks associated with overtraining.

Reduced Risks of Psychological Impairment

It is widely recognized that overtraining leads to decreased quality of sleep, insomnia, anxiety, and depression, all of which are factors that increase the risks of psychological impairment. Overtraining increases the levels of epinephrine and norepinephrine, causing unwanted increases in heart rate and blood pressure, both of which are detrimental to physical and psychological well-being. In addition to the known detrimental psychological side effects, long-term epinephrine and norepinephrine elevation decreases testosterone levels, leading to decreased muscle and stunted or inhibited training adaptations.

Improved Performance

Intentional undertraining can improve performance when a resistance training program focuses on delivering consistent timing cues to muscle clocks and muscles. Exercise training and programming cues can initiate in advance of a workout session the molecular actions associated with desired muscle performance, increasing the efficacy of a resistance training session. When muscles know what to expect in advance, they are ready for performance, maximizing the performance benefits of time in the gym instead of relying on overload only to stimulate the molecular mechanisms associated with muscle growth, strength, and power outcomes.

Less Recovery Time

Muscle contractility is affected by resistance training; therefore, muscles need at least 48 h to return to baseline levels of strength after a high-intensity (>80% 1RM) resistance training session (2). Muscles fatigued due to overtraining require more recovery time than do muscles that are less fatigued. In any case, muscles must be given no less than 48 h to recover after moderate- to high-intensity resistance exercise. The intensity of resistance training aside, muscle contractility can also be affected by the frequency and volume of resistance training, programming variables that when used in excess result in overtraining, and the need for increased recovery times; strategic intentional undertraining, however, can yield shorter recovery times.

Differentiated Programming

Novel and strategic programming solutions are needed to modulate training load to avoid overusing only increased volume and intensity. A way to change resistance training methods is to change the training mode. In this case, the suggestion is to use both unilateral and bilateral movements where mostly bilateral exercises are used. One study compared the efficacy of unilateral to bilateral resistance training in young experienced basketball players (4).

In this study, resistance training programs lasted 6 weeks and included 3 sets of either unilateral or bilateral 90° back squats. Repetitions were performed until the power output dropped to below 10% of maximum power output. In addition to the back squat exercise, both groups did 2 sets of 5 unilateral or bilateral drop jumps and 2 sets of 5 unilateral or bilateral countermovement jumps. The experimental difference was whether the participants did unilateral or bilateral resistance training. Researchers measured the effects of bilateral versus unilateral training on single-leg power output, between-limb imbalance, bilateral deficit, change of direction, and linear sprinting and jumping performance. Performance was assessed before and after the 6-week training program with an incremental bilateral and unilateral squat-load test, a multiple-change of direction test (V-cut test), a 15 m (16.4 yd) sprint test with one 180° change of direction performed with both right and left legs, a 25 m (27 yd) sprint test (5 m [5.5 yd] and 15 m [16.4 yd] split time), and a countermovement jump test.

Results showed significant improvements in 180° right change of direction, bilateral and unilateral maximum power output, 25 m (27 yd) sprint test, and countermovement jump in both groups. However, the unilateral training group performed better than the bilateral training group on the tests that measured 180° left change of direction, maximum power output with right and left legs individually, between-limb imbalance, and bilateral deficit. These results are significant because what they showed is that both training programs substantially improved most of the physical fitness tests, but unilateral training reduced between-limb asymmetry and achieved greater enhancements in actions that mostly required applying muscle force unilaterally. The results suggest that unilateral training is more effective than bilateral training for specific outcomes and is a viable way to differentiate programming versus strictly increasing training load.

Activity–Rest Interval Focused

Activity–rest intervals are the periods of time that the body spends in activity versus rest. For most people, activity–rest intervals are fairly predictable, relying on environmental cues such as light–dark cycles associated with the time of day during a 24 h cycle. Light–dark cycles dictate sleep versus activity for most people; however, as discussed earlier, sleep is disrupted by high-intensity training, which throws off the body's natural activity–rest cycles.

Activity–rest patterns may vary from person to person based on factors such as individual chronotype (whether someone is described as a morning or a night person) but tend to be fairly predictable in exercise training and programming settings. Workouts normally are scheduled during the day in alignment with most people's natural activity–rest patterns, and consistently scheduled exercise training delivers cues to muscles about these activity–rest patterns, allowing them to prep in advance of training. Intentional undertraining uses the body's natural activity–rest intervals to build regularly scheduled workout programs that rely on timing cues to muscle clocks to increase the efficacy of training versus increasing training loads only.

Intermittent Rest Focused

Intermittent rest or alternate days off provides muscles with timing cues. Specifically, with intermittent rest, both the frequency of training and the activity–rest intervals according to light–dark cycles provide muscles with timing cues consistent within a 24 h period.

As an exercise programming strategy, intermittent rest is taking two nonconsecutive days off per week in contrast to a traditional week-on and weekend-off training schedule. This suggestion is consistent with the fact that muscle clocks are on a 24 h cycle regardless of the day of the week and is based on the assumption that staying within a 24 h day schedule every day provides muscles with consistent timing cues about the time of day and activity–rest cycles.

The efficacy of alternate-day resistance training methods was examined in one study in which researchers compared the effects of compound training (strength and power workouts on alternate days) to complex resistance training (strength and power training sets within a single session) on muscle strength, high-speed movement performance, and muscle composition (10). During the study, 18 young men completed either compound or complex resistance training three times per week for 6 weeks using the bench press, leg press, Smith machine box squat, and jumping exercises. Before and after the training period, jumping and throwing performance and maximum bench press, leg press, and Smith machine box squat strength were tested. The structure of the vastus lateralis and gastrocnemius muscles were assessed via ultrasound imaging. Additional information on the morphology of the vastus lateralis was collected using muscle biopsies.

The results of the study showed that jumping and throwing performance, a measure of muscle power, increased only with compound training. For the bench press, leg press, and Smith machine box squat, absolute strength increased with both compound and complex training, but muscle fiber cross-sectional areas increased only after complex training. The results showed jumping and throwing performance were superior after the compound training program and suggested that at least short-term strength and power training on alternate days is more effective for enhancing lower-limb and whole-body power than a same session strength and power training program. However, it is imperative to mention that complex training resulted in greater strength and fiber hypertrophy improvements than alternate day training.

Overall, these results suggest that compound training is a viable training method for power development in the upper and lower body and is a way to mitigate the risks associated with overtraining. Compound training paradigms are also consistent with recommendations for keeping muscles and muscle clocks on a 24 h schedule with clear activity–rest patterns and programming for alternate days of rest.

Workout Routines

As mentioned earlier, one way to avoid overtraining is to change the way training is performed. One study compared how two different resistance training programs affected athletic performance in 16-year-old male soccer players (6). It is important to note that the study was done at a critical point during the athletes' competitive season, and competition time would add to the total training load. The athletes were assigned to either a control group, a group that performed standard resistance training, or a group that performed contrast resistance training (alternating a heavy exercise with a light load exercise). Contrast resistance training is particularly relevant to modulating training loads because it uses a light load in place of a heavy or moderate load; therefore, the volume is relatively high, but the overall intensity is moderate.

Each resistance training group performed either standard or contrast training twice per week for 8 weeks. Athletic performance was measured before and after the resistance training programs using eight tests: the 40 m (44 yd) sprint, 4 × 5 m (5 yd) sprint, 9-3-6-3-9 m (10-3-6.5-3-10 yd) sprint with 180° turns, 9-3-6-3-9 m (10-3-6.5-3-10 yd) sprint with backward and forward running, repeated shuttle sprint, repeated change of direction, squat jump, and countermovement jump. The most significant finding was that both resistance training programs improved performance in all sprint tests when compared to the control group. The standard resistance training group and the contrast resistance training group both improved significantly in the sprint test with 180° turns, sprint with backward and forward running, and 4 × 5 m (5 yd) sprints relative to the control group. In support of the contrast strength training method, the sprint 4 × 5 m (5 yd) performance and the repeated change of direction tests also improved compared to the standard resistance training group and the control group. The standard jump and countermovement jump height, both indicators of muscle power, increased significantly in both the standard and contrast resistance training groups.

Again, it is important to note that the study was conducted during competition season, and therefore playing time contributed to overall training load frequency, volume, and intensity and affected the likelihood of fatigue and overtraining, which could have influenced test results. However, the study conclusion remains the same: During the competitive season, some measures of athletic performance in young male soccer players were improved more by 8 weeks of contrast resistance training than by standard resistance training. This supports the programming suggestion that differential modes and training methods should be used to counter the risk of overtraining.

Recovery Focused

Programming modifications and suggestions to best use and manipulate training variables to exploit the concept of intentional undertraining should be recovery focused. Alternate training days (compound training) allows for minimal recovery between training sessions, but, more important, it is consistent with the desire of muscle clocks to stay on a 24 h schedule. Alternate training day programming has been shown effective for muscle power development. Specifically, one study showed that jumping and throwing performances were superior after a compound training program versus complex resistance training, suggesting that it is more effective to alternate strength and power training days to enhance lower-limb and whole-body power than to program strength and power training into the same session (10).

Another study compared the time course of elbow flexor muscle recovery after multijoint versus single-joint exercises in highly resistance-trained men (9). A total of 16 men ranging in age from 20 to 30 years old performed, in a counterbalanced order, 8 sets of unilateral seated rows (using a 10 RM load) and 8 sets of unilateral biceps preacher curls (also using a 10 RM load) with the contralateral arm. Maximum isometric peak torque and delayed-onset muscle soreness (DOMS) were recorded at baseline before the training session, 10 min into the training session, and 24, 48, 72, and 96 h after each exercise session.

There was a significant decrease in elbow flexor peak torque 10 min after both the multijoint and single-joint exercise sessions. However, peak torque decrease was greater after the single-joint exercise session when compared with the multijoint exercise session. In addition, elbow flexor peak torque was lower than baseline 24 h after the single-joint exercise session, whereas peak torque returned to baseline 24 h after the multijoint exercise session. Compared with baseline, DOMS increased at 24, 48, and 72 h after the single-joint exercise session. However, DOMS returned to baseline levels after 72 h following the multijoint exercise session. In addition, DOMS after the single-joint exercise session was greater than after the multijoint exercise session at 24, 48, and 72 h after exercise. The data suggest that after a resistance training session, highly resistance-trained men experience dissimilar elbow flexor strength recovery between single-joint and multijoint exercises. Likewise, elbow flexor DOMS is greater and takes longer to recover after single-joint exercise sessions.

Based on the results of this study, the programming recommendation is to stay away from single-joint exercises when fatigue is a concern. DOMS represents microscopic tears in muscles that require adequate recovery time to repair. DOMS causes a series of events, including microscopic damage to muscle fibers, that prevent strength gains. One study has shown that when DOMS happens, strength decreases over the same time in beginning exercisers (1).

Other reasons to focus on recovery time include substrate depletion and protein breakdown (3), which occur during prolonged muscle work. These physiological processes occur during resistance training and reduce available substrates and protein for muscle function and growth that would otherwise be used to increase muscle performance.

Conclusion

Intentional undertraining is in direct contrast to resistance training methods that focus on increasing training volume and intensity only. The most obvious problem with high-intensity and high-volume training methods is that they are prone to exhaust muscles, leading to prolonged fatigue and overtraining. In contrast to resistance training methods that are likely to result in poor recovery and cause overtraining, intentional undertraining focuses on resistance training methods that modulate training loads to include low to moderate loads and adequate recovery times.

Intentional undertraining is a viable training method when timing cues, such as consistently scheduled exercise training and programming and activity–rest patterns, are used as primary exercise programming variables. The assumption is that when a resistance training program that focuses on timing is consistently performed, it provides muscle clocks with critical information that they can use to anticipate workout sessions and click on the molecular actions associated with improved muscle performance in advance, leading to improved performance. This is in contrast to relying on overloading muscles through only high-intensity and high-volume training methods. Intentional undertraining as a training method is in alignment with exercise programming strategies that focus on monitoring training load in relationship to the timing cues delivered to muscle clocks, varying resistance training methods, and being aware of the body's differential responses to timing cues and alternative programming methods that lead to improved performance outcomes.

7 | Using Muscle Clocks to Train for Strength

Muscle clocks need consistency to establish rhythms and initiate the physiological changes associated with muscle strength. One way to do that is to use biomechanically similar paired exercises to program for muscle strength outcomes. This chapter presents suggested paired workouts and training programs that use the exercises detailed in chapter 4. Single-session workouts and long-term programming suggestions are made with the intent to improve muscle strength and overall muscle performance.

Paired Exercise Resistance Training Model

A paired exercise resistance training model is a way to design workouts using two biomechanically similar exercises. What makes the programming method unique is the use of exercises that use similar muscles and muscle groups and joint actions. Using similar paired exercises is comparable to superset methods and is not a new way to train; what is new, however, is that the exercises are used in a unique way to provide critical timing cues to muscle clocks about the mode of exercises, exercise frequency, exercise mechanics, and exercise volume and intensity.

In addition, it is worth noting that paired exercises, aside from providing time cues to muscle clocks, are effective because they use the same muscles or muscle groups in different ways, recruiting different muscles fibers. Hence exercises that look mechanically similar and work the same or similar muscles or muscle groups nevertheless work muscles differently, increasing the work done by targeted muscles and improving muscle performance.

Use of Multijoint Exercises

A biomechanically paired exercise programming method relies on the use of multijoint exercises. Multijoint exercises, including all-body power exercises such as the snatch and other common compound (multijoint) exercises such as squats and lunges, are the foundation for the biomechanically similar paired training method. Compound exercises are effective because they use the most muscles and muscle groups during the exercise. For that reason, they are the most popular choices for use in both general fitness and athletic training settings. Compound exercises are also known to release high amounts of both testosterone and human growth hormone (HGH) into the bloodstream to facilitate muscle growth, strength, and power development.

One study compared the effects of equal-volume (amount of training per session and week) single-joint and multijoint resistance training on $\dot{V}O_2$max, muscle strength, and body composition in trained men (7). A total of 36 participants were divided into two groups. In the first group, participants performed single-joint exercises only, including the dumbbell fly, knee extension, knee flexion, pec deck, biceps curl, incline dumbbell fly, abdominal curl, lateral raise, pull-over, rear deltoid fly, cable elbow extension, and calf raise. In the second group, participants performed multijoint exercises only, including the bench press, deadlift, squat, leg press, shoulder press, lat pulldown, and seated row. The exercises in each session varied throughout the week for both groups. The total work *volume* (repetitions × sets × load) was the same for each group. Exercises were performed three times a week for 8 weeks. Both groups were tested for $\dot{V}O_2$max and body composition. Subjects were also tested for 1RM on the bench press, knee extension, and squat before training began and after the training period.

The results showed that both multijoint and single-joint only exercise groups decreased body fat and increased fat-free mass with no difference between them. While both groups significantly increased cardiorespiratory fitness and maximal muscle strength, the improvements in the multijoint exercise group were higher than the single-joint exercise group in $\dot{V}O_2$max, bench press 1RM, knee extension 1RM, and squat 1RM. The study showed that when total work volume was equated, resistance training programs involving multijoint exercises appear to be more effective for improving muscle strength and maximal oxygen consumption uptake than programs involving single-joint exercises only, but no differences in improvements in body fat or fat-free mass were found.

The results of this study confirm that while single-joint exercises have a role in resistance training programs to improve body composition and play a supporting role, compound exercises are the better choice for muscle strength improvements. Compound exercises are better suited to improve all elements of performance, including muscle endurance, strength, and power. However, compound exercises do have several limitations: They are limited by motor coordination and the exerciser's previous experience and can lack muscle focus if the mechanics are not correct.

As discussed in chapter 5, it can take a week to months to years to master complex skills, and compound exercises are considered complex. It may be difficult to master the mechanics correctly. Therefore, compound movements are typically reserved for exercisers who have training experience. Only the most experienced exercisers should attempt all-body power lifts, especially when heavy loads are lifted.

The training principle of specificity states that only the muscles used will respond to the training demands. As specificity relates to compound movements, the nature of all-body lifts and many muscle group exercises can be a limiting factor to their effectiveness. For example, a compound exercise such as a squat is great for the gluteus maximus and quadriceps but less so for the hamstrings. If an exerciser needs to target the hamstrings specifically, he or she would be better served by a targeted knee flexion exercise such as the prone (face down) machine lying hamstring curl.

Complimentary Use of Single-Joint Exercises

The efficacy of compound movements cannot be denied for overall muscle performance and transfer of motor skills from training sessions to athletic performance and everyday life. However, compound movements can be limited by the fact that they do not focus work on specific muscles. Therefore, a way to complement compound exercises and improve training efficacy is to use single-joint exercises in biomechanically paired training routines.

Also termed *isolation exercises* because they isolate the work to a specific muscle or muscle group, single-joint exercises are a great way to apply the training principle of specificity to improve the performance of a targeted muscle group. Popular for developing muscle hypertrophy and inducing positive body composition changes, single-joint exercises are not a sole solution but are part of a bigger and comprehensive programming method.

In the use of a biomechanically similar paired exercise workout, isolation exercises are paired with compound exercises. For example, a knee extension is paired with a front squat to target the quadriceps muscles.

Although most workouts and programs start with a compound exercise and build from there, another easy way to build a session is based on a single-joint exercise. For example, a common need is to develop the strength of a smaller muscle, such as the triceps. Therefore it is prudent to start a session with exercises that target the smaller muscle. A session focusing on the triceps first would start with a triceps kickback (elbow extension) and then add a biomechanically similar compound exercise such as a triceps dip that uses elbow extension to propel the body up.

Pairing Biomechanically Similar Exercises

Pairing biomechanically similar exercises is a formula to help exercisers and professionals choose exercises and design workouts and long-term programs. The first step is to focus on a specific muscle group or joint action.

The mode of exercise is a critical programming cue to entrain muscle clocks. Muscle clocks look for biomechanical similarity. The biomechanical similarity is the degree to which two exercises use similar motions and is determined by the primary muscles used and the associated joint actions. Exercise-specific timing cues are based on the primary muscles trained and the primary joints and muscle actions performed. For example, a triceps pushdown is similar to a triceps overhead press, because both exercises use the triceps muscles as the primary muscle and elbow flexion and extension as the primary joint action.

Biomechanical similarity is a training method that pairs two exercises that are alike. Pairing exercises that use similar muscles or muscle groups in similar joint patterns provide muscle clocks with invaluable timing cues. The similarity of movements is an entrainment cue that can help muscle clocks establish a schedule and anticipate upcoming training sessions. With biomechanically similar exercises providing consistent clues, muscle clocks learn when to click on the molecular actions associated with resistance training during each 24 h period.

Same or Similar Muscles Used

Biomechanically similar exercises work the same or similar muscles. However, the goal of a paired exercise training model is to activate the same muscles in two different ways. Different movement patterns use different bundles of muscle fibers within the same muscle. For example, both a back squat and leg press train the muscles of the legs and hips. However, each exercise activates slightly different bundles of muscle fibers within the same muscles, differing how they are used. The end programming result is a more comprehensive workout for the entire muscle group. Figures 7.1 and 7.2 illustrate biomechanically paired exercises using the bent-over row and the pullover.

FIGURE 7.1   Bent-over row: (*a*) starting position; (*b*) ending position.

FIGURE 7.2   Pullover: (*a*) starting position; (*b*) ending position.

Same or Similar Joint Actions Used

Pairing exercises that use similar joint actions establish biomechanical similarity. For example, the paired exercises can use similar joint actions, such as shoulder elevation and depression or hip abduction and adduction, providing important exercise training and programming cues to muscle clocks.

Exercise-specific timing cues are based on the primary joints used and muscle actions performed. The snatch (figure 7.3) and front squat (figure 7.4) exercises illustrate the concept of similar joint actions with two different exercises.

FIGURE 7.3 Snatch: (*a*) starting position; (*b*) ending "catch" position.

FIGURE 7.4 Front squat: (*a*) starting position; (*b*) bottom position.

Timing Cues

Exercise-specific timing cues are based on the primary muscles trained and the primary joints and muscle actions performed. For example, as described earlier, a triceps pushdown is similar to a triceps overhead press, because both exercises use the triceps muscles as the primary muscle and elbow flexion and extension as the primary joint action. With a regular schedule, the similarity of movement between the two triceps exercises provides muscle clocks with cues about training mode and type(s) of exercises to anticipate in an upcoming training session.

Use of Biomechanically Similar Exercises

When the muscle and joint actions of different exercises are matched, the exercises are considered biomechanically similar. However, the exercises don't necessarily have to target the same muscles. Figures 7.5 and 7.6 show how to pair two exercises, the shoulder press and shoulder shrug, that use the same muscles and joint but have different joint actions. This is an effective way to program an exercise session based on the primary joints used.

FIGURE 7.5   Shoulder press: (*a*) starting position; (*b*) ending position.

FIGURE 7.6   Shoulder shrug: (*a*) starting position; (*b*) ending position.

Testosterone Levels and Release

Testosterone levels naturally fluctuate throughout the day. Muscle clocks are aware of these fluctuations and account for them when setting and resetting 24 h biological rhythms. Testosterone levels are highest in the morning and then begin to level off between 4 and 6 p.m., decreasing after that. The presumed reason for high testosterone in the morning is that testosterone is needed during the day and not needed for sleep. The daily fluctuation in testosterone levels is a perfect example of synchrony within the human body—natural occurring levels of a hormone required for muscle strength and power are highest early in the day when internal clocks anticipate activity and decrease ahead of anticipated rest.

Although testosterone levels change throughout the day naturally at times that are consistent with activity versus rest in most people, testosterone levels can be manipulated by other factors such as resistance training. Resistance training influences testosterone levels during and after a workout session (10).

More specific than resistance training only, testosterone levels respond differently to various exercises such as the deadlift versus the good morning exercise. For example, a deadlift (figure 7.7), an all-body exercise and stressor, releases more testosterone into the bloodstream than a good morning (figure 7.8), a single-joint exercise that uses one joint (the hips) and fewer muscles. The difference in the amount of testosterone released is related to the volume of muscle mass used and the overall intensity differences between the two exercises. Whereas a deadlift uses the single largest muscle in the body (the gluteus maximus) and the largest muscle group (the quadriceps), the good morning uses only one joint and fewer muscles. Clearly, the deadlift is a more intense exercise than the good morning and would be a more effective exercise for releasing testosterone and HGH. Therefore, it can be argued that the deadlift is a better cue for muscle clocks than the good morning, although they are biomechanically similar.

FIGURE 7.7 Deadlift: (*a*) starting position; (*b*) ending position.

FIGURE 7.8 Good morning: (*a*) starting position; (*b*) ending position.

Human Growth Hormone Release

Just like testosterone, HGH is released into the bloodstream during exercise. Compound exercises such as squats and deadlifts that use multiple joints and large muscle groups are the most effective in releasing HGH (3). Also, eccentric actions cause more HGH release than concentric contractions (3).

Cortisol Release

Because exercise is a source of stress, it stimulates the release of cortisol, a stress hormone, into the bloodstream. Cortisol is released in response to emotional stress (such as pain, anger, and fear) and physical work (such as scheduled resistance training). Like most of the body's chemicals, cortisol also has its own natural daily rhythm. Natural cortisol levels are at their highest around 8 a.m. and lowest at 3 to 4 a.m., indicating a pattern similar to testosterone, which indicates a need for cortisol while awake and alert and less of a need while resting and sleeping. Similar to other biochemical markers in the body such as testosterone and HGH, cortisol levels fluctuate throughout the day and also increase or decrease in response to their environment.

Because cortisol is a chemical that is released on its own time and during scheduled resistance training, it is a timing cue for muscle clocks to anticipate upcoming exercise sessions. Cortisol release would be similar between two large compound exercises such as the squat and the deadlift, but it would be less for a single-joint exercise such as a biceps curl or triceps extension.

Resistance Training Programming

Finally, and most important to sport and fitness practitioners, are the timing cues that muscle clocks get from well-structured scheduled exercise training and programming. What is important to remember is that muscle clocks use exercise training and programming cues to help do their job to regulate muscle performance and synchronize muscles with other body systems. Timing cues are used to reprogram muscle clocks to aid in things such as metabolic function related to muscle performance, sleep, and recovery. To facilitate positive changes in muscle associated with performance, paired biomechanically similar exercises should be used.

Using Mode (Type of Exercise) to Design Workouts

In chapter 3, the mode of exercise was defined as the type of exercise performed, as broad as the difference between cardiovascular training such as cycling and resistance training with weights. As discussed in chapter 2, interference occurs when cardiovascular exercise is performed less than 3 h before resistance training.

Although leaving adequate time between competing modes of exercise is critical and worth mentioning again, here mode is discussed within the context of resistance training only and biomechanical similarity. Mode of resistance training is whether an exercise is a single-joint or multijoint exercise, for example, and which joints and muscle actions are used. Pairing exercises that have similar muscle and joint actions is critical to providing muscle clocks with consistent cues about upcoming exercise sessions.

All-Body Power Exercises

All-body power exercises use many large muscle groups at the same time and, therefore, are considered all-body exercises. All-body power exercises are advanced exercises and are suggested for experienced exercisers only.

Lower- and Upper-Body Exercises

Lower-body exercises use the muscles and joints of only the lower body to complete the exercise. Upper-body exercises use the muscles and joints of only the upper body to complete the exercise. In a biomechanically paired workout session, with the exception of all-body power exercises, either muscles and joints of the upper or lower body are used to match biomechanics of the two different exercises.

Bilateral and Unilateral Exercises

When designing a biomechanically paired exercise workout, it is possible to use unilateral, bilateral, or both types of exercises in one session. A unilateral exercise such as a side lunge can be paired with a bilateral machine seated knee extension. Although one is unilateral and the other bilateral, both exercises use knee extension and flexion and use the quadriceps muscles.

Unilateral training is a great way to work each side of the body equally, but it also has a unique advantage of making the external core muscles work more than bilaterally. One study compared core muscle activation among three different row exercises (free weight bent-over row, seated cable row, and machine row) (9). Each exercise was done unilaterally and bilaterally at equal effort levels. A total of 15 resistance-trained men ranging in age from 26 to 81 years old participated. All exercises were done in random order. For the erector spinae and multifidus muscles, electromyographic (EMG) activity showed that muscle output was 60% to 63% and 74% to 78% of the effort for the unilateral machine versus the bilateral exercise for the cable rows. External oblique activity during the bilateral exercises was 37% to 41% of the effort for unilateral exercises, indicating external core muscles worked more during unilateral work than bilateral work. In unilateral cable and machine row exercises, the EMG activities in external oblique and multifidus were

50% to 57% and 70% to 73% of the free weight row. EMG activity in the erector spinae was greater for a bilateral free weight row than for bilateral machine and unilateral free weight rows. For the rectus abdominis, there were no significant differences between the unilateral and bilateral exercises. In conclusion, the free weight row caused greater muscle activity in the erector spinae, both bilaterally and unilaterally, and in the multifidus unilaterally than the machine row. The unilateral performance of exercises activated the external oblique more than bilateral performance, regardless of exercise. Generally the bilateral performance of exercises provided higher erector spinae and multifidus muscle activity compared to unilateral performance.

The sum of forces produced by each limb in a unilateral exercise is generally greater than that produced by them together in a bilateral condition. Therefore, it can be speculated that performing unilateral strength exercises may produce better training workloads and subsequently greater neuromuscular adaptations when compared to bilateral training. Hence the purpose of one study was to compare neuromuscular adaptations between unilateral and bilateral training in the knee extensor muscles (2). A total of 43 recreationally active young women were allocated to a control, unilateral, or bilateral training group. Each group, excluding the control group, performed resistance training two times per week for 12 weeks. Knee extension 1RM, maximal isometric strength, muscle electrical activity, and muscle thickness were measured before and after the training period. Muscle strength was measured in unilateral (right + left) and bilateral tests.

The results showed that both the unilateral and bilateral training groups increased their unilateral 1RM, bilateral 1RM, and isometric strength. The unilateral training group demonstrated greater unilateral isometric strength increase than the bilateral group, and only the unilateral group increased muscle electrical activity. Muscle thickness increased similarly for both training groups. Neither group exhibited pretesting 1RM bilateral deficit values, but at posttesting, the unilateral group showed a significant bilateral deficit, whereas the bilateral training group showed a significant bilateral facilitation. Thus performing unilateral or bilateral exercises was not a decisive factor for improving muscle performance and bilateral muscle strength; however, unilateral training facilitated unilateral specific strength gains.

Agonist–Antagonist Exercises

A helpful way to think about the body during resistance training is to think of it as a cable or pulley system. Pulleys work with two opposing series of cables or a similar object like a rope working opposite one another but in a complementary way. With a typical cable system, when one side is tense, the other is relaxed.

The concept of cable systems may be easier to visualize when thinking of it in terms of the more popular concept of strength training agonist–antagonist muscle groups or functional opposite muscles such as the triceps and biceps muscles. For both stretching and strength training, the principle of agonist–antagonist muscles is the same. During strength training, when the biceps muscle contracts, the triceps muscle relaxes and vice versa. This complementary action allows for greater contraction of the targeted muscles.

Pairing agonist–antagonist muscle exercises during training is a popular way to train and design workouts. An example of a biomechanically paired agonist–antagonist exercise set is the machine seated leg extension with the machine lying knee flexion. Both exercises use knee extension and flexion to execute the movements, but the knee extension targets the quadriceps, while the knee flexion targets the hamstrings, the quadriceps's functional opposite or antagonist muscle.

Intensity

Intensity is how hard the exerciser is working. With resistance training, the intensity is represented by a percent of an exerciser's 1RM effort. It is assumed that the higher the exercise intensity, the greater the positive outcomes. However, there are other exercise training and programming factors to consider besides intensity.

In one study, researchers looked at the muscular adaptations after 2 and 4 weeks of 80% 1RM versus 30% 1RM resistance training to failure (4). The intent of the study was to determine the different hypertrophic and strength adaptations of different resistance training intensities: 80% versus 30% 1RM. A total of 15 untrained young men were randomly assigned to either a high-load or low-load resistance training program. Each group of participants completed forearm flexion resistance training to failure three times per week for 4 consecutive weeks. Forearm flexor muscle thickness, maximal voluntary isometric contraction, and 1RM were determined at baseline, 2, and 4 weeks of training. Muscle thickness, represented as cross-sectional muscle area and indicating muscle hypertrophy, increased from baseline to week 2 and to week 4 for both the 80% and 30% 1RM training groups. Maximal voluntary isometric contraction increased from week 2 to week 4, and 1RM increased from baseline to weeks 2 and 4 in only the 80% 1RM group.

Resistance training to failure, notably not a common training method, at 80% versus 30% 1RM caused similar muscle hypertrophy or growth, but only training at 80% 1RM increased muscle strength. However, it is important to note that untrained young men were used in the study, and it is expected that early neuromuscular and muscle hypertrophy improvements would be seen with almost any measurable resistance. The important takeaway message here is that the higher intensity training at 80% 1RM increased strength while training at 30% 1RM did not.

Volume

Volume is the amount of exercise done during a training session. In resistance training, the volume is the total number of repetitions and sets completed within one session. The session volume might also be combined with the training frequency to reflect the total amount of work done over a week.

A study on resistance training volume compared the response of performing 1, 3, and 5 sets of resistance training exercises on muscle performance and muscle hypertrophy (8). In this study, 48 men with no weight training experience were assigned to either a 1-set, 3-set, or 5-set exercise group or a control group. All exercise groups performed the bench press, front lat pulldown, shoulder press, and leg press three times per week for 6 months.

After 6 months, the 5RM (the most weight that can be lifted for five repetitions) for all exercise groups increased in the bench press, front lat pulldown, shoulder press, and leg press. However the 5RM increases in the bench press and front lat pulldown were significantly greater in the 5-set group compared to the 1- and 3-set groups, indicating that volume of training up to 5 sets positively affected bench press and front lat pulldown muscle strength.

The 20RM load (an indicator of muscle endurance) for the bench press significantly increased in the 3- and 5-set groups. The increase in muscle endurance was significant for both the 3- and 5-set groups versus the 1-set group, and the 5-set group increased significantly more than the 3-set group, indicating the positive effects of training volume on muscle endurance during a bench press. The front lat pulldown 20RM load increased in all training groups, with the 5-set group showing a significantly greater increase than the 1-set group, again indicating the value of increased volume to muscle endurance.

Training volume also positively affects muscle hypertrophy. The 3- and 5-set groups significantly increased elbow flexor muscle thickness, with the 5-set group increase being significantly greater than the other two training groups. All three exercise training groups decreased body fat percentage, increased fat-free mass, and improved vertical jump ability (a measure of muscle power), with no differences among the groups. The results of the study confirm a dose-response effect for the number of sets per exercise and multiple sets as superior when compared to a single-set per exercise for strength gains, muscle endurance, and upper-arm muscle hypertrophy.

In another study on the efficacy of training volume on muscle performance (1), German volume training (GVT), or the 10-set method, was examined. GVT has been used for decades by experienced weightlifters to increase muscle mass. Therefore, the purpose of this study was to investigate the effects of a traditional GVT (10 sets) versus a modified GVT (5 sets) program on muscular hypertrophy and strength. For this study, 19 healthy men were randomly assigned to 6 weeks of 10 sets or 5 sets of 10 repetitions for specific multijoint resistance training exercises. Exercises were split into a regular routine and performed three times per week. Total and regional lean body mass, muscle thickness, and muscle strength were measured before and after the training program.

The results showed that across both groups (10 sets and 5 sets), there were significant increases in lean body mass. However, greater increases in trunk and arm lean body mass favored the 5-set group. No significant increases were found for leg lean body mass or measures of muscle thickness between groups. Significant increases were found between groups for muscular strength, with greater increases in the 5-set group for bench press and lat pulldown. Based on the results of the study, it appears that traditional GVT (10 set) programming is no more effective for increasing muscle hypertrophy and strength than performing 5 sets per exercise. To maximize muscle hypertrophy from training, 4 to 6 sets per exercise are recommended, as it seems muscle performance will plateau beyond this set range, and more sets may even result in overtraining.

Work–Rest Periods

Work–rest periods are a vital timing cue to muscle clocks in determining what to anticipate each 24 h period. Using exercise training and programming, it is possible to entrain muscles to know what to expect during such a period.

The most common way to think about work–rest periods and their relation to muscle clock entrainment is on a larger scale, like hours during a 24 h period. However work–rest periods on a smaller scale, like between and within resistance training sets, also relate to timing and muscle performance. One study set out to determine if rest intervals within a set, termed *intraset rest breaks,* produced greater increases in muscle strength and power compared to traditional rest breaks between sets (5). The study examined 22 men ranging in age from 25 to 65 years who were assigned to 12 weeks of resistance training using either traditional between-set rest breaks or intraset (within-set) rest breaks. Exercise order and intensity were the same between the two groups. The only variable that changed was the length of rest breaks and when rest periods occurred, either within or between sets. Strength, defined as 1RM on the bench press and squat, and power output (60% 1RM) on the bench press and squat were measured before the study began and again after 4, 8, and 12 weeks of resistance training. The results showed that the 60 s intraset rest breaks resulted in statistically significant greater strength gains and power output in the bench press and nearing a statistical significance difference in the squat for strength and power than the 120 s traditional between-set rest breaks. These findings are important because they indicate that smaller intraset rest intervals are more effective for muscle performance, specifically strength and power improvement, than longer between-set rests.

Vary Patterns of Activation

As discussed in earlier chapters, muscle confusion is interference theory at a microscopic level. It is the molecular explanation for why concurrent cardiovascular training and resistance training interferes with resistance training outcomes. When two competing modes of exercise, such as resistance and cardiovascular endurance training, are done within 30 min of each other, muscles get confused at the molecular level, and strength gains are adversely affected.

Although it is known that different modes of training, such as cardiovascular and resistance training, compete at the cellular level, it is still important that muscles are trained in a variety of ways. In the case of resistance training, the focus is on using different exercise biomechanics instead of different modes of exercise to vary workload. Biomechanically similar exercises work the same or similar muscles, but they activate muscles in different ways. Varying movement patterns use different bundles of muscle fibers within the same muscle. For example, both a back squat and leg press train the muscles of the legs and hips. However, each exercise activates slightly different bundles of muscle fibers within the same muscles. The end programming result is a more comprehensive workout for the entire muscle group.

Muscle fibers within a muscle are recruited in order from slow-twitch fibers to fast-twitch fibers. As a rule, the faster the movement and the more strength required to completely execute the exercise, the more fast-twitch fibers are used. In many movements, such as walking, fast-twitch fibers are minimally involved. However, a plyometric push-up and a heavy loaded bench press recruit many fast-twitch fibers. Factors that determine the extent of muscle fiber recruitment and release order are the mechanics of the exercise, intensity (weight, the speed of contraction, or both), and range of motion.

For example, a traditional walking lunge with no weight will recruit fewer fast-twitch fibers overall, even though the mechanics are the same as a heavy loaded split squat. When external weight is added, increasing the intensity of the exercise, a greater number of fast-twitch fibers are recruited. They will also be released later in the sequence to sustain forceful contraction throughout the entire range of motion (to avoid getting stuck under a barbell during a bench press, for example).

Resistance Exercise Pairing Routines

It is not enough to simply pair biomechanically similar exercises and superset them. Intensity and volume of each workout session must also be considered carefully. One study compared high-load (80% 1RM) sets, low-load (30% 1RM) sets, and a single high-load set plus additional drop sets descending to a low load without recovery and their effect on muscle endurance, hypertrophy, and strength in nine untrained young men (6). Each group was randomly assigned to one of three methods: 3 sets of high-load (HL, 80% 1RM) resistance exercise, 3 sets of low-load (LL, 30% 1RM) resistance exercise, or a single high-load set with additional drop sets descending to a low-load set. Exercises were performed two or three days per week for 8 weeks.

It is very important to note that the mean training time per session, including recovery intervals, was lowest in the single high-load training group. The results showed that the elbow flexor muscle cross-sectional area, an indicator of hypertrophy, increased similarly in all three training groups. Maximum isometric and 1RM strength of the elbow flexors increased from before to after the study only in the high-load (80% 1RM) and single high-load drop set conditions, indicating the value of the intensity of training on muscle strength development. Muscular endurance, measured by maximum number of repetitions at 30% 1RM, increased only in the low-load (30% 1RM) and single high-load drop set conditions, demonstrating the value of low loads to muscle endurance. Overall, the results of the study showed that a single high-load set with a descending drop set to a low-load set resistance training program can simultaneously increase muscle hypertrophy, strength, and endurance in untrained young men when compared to 3-set training models. These results are important because they show that even with less time spent training and with lower training volumes, a mixed-intensity protocol is as effective as a typical resistance training protocol that uses only high or low loads.

Tables 7.1 through 7.7 show a variety of pairing routines.

TABLE 7.1 Pairing Routine for All-Body Power Exercises

Exercise	Reps	Resistance	Between-set rest break
Power clean	4-6	65%-85% 1RM	30 s-4 min
Power shrug	4-6	65%-85% 1RM	30 s-4 min
Power clean	4-6	65%-85% 1RM	30 s-4 min
Power shrug	4-6	65%-85% 1RM	30 s-4 min
Power clean	4-6	65%-85% 1RM	30 s-4 min
Power shrug	4-6	65%-85% 1RM	30 s-4 min

TABLE 7.2 Pairing Routine for Bilateral Lower-Body Exercises

Exercise	Reps	Resistance	Between-set rest break
Back squat	4-6	65%-85% 1RM	30 s-4 min
Leg press	4-6	65%-85% 1RM	30 s-4 min
Back squat	4-6	65%-85% 1RM	30 s-4 min
Leg press	4-6	65%-85% 1RM	30 s-4 min
Back squat	4-6	65%-85% 1RM	30 s-4 min
Leg press	4-6	65%-85% 1RM	30 s-4 min

TABLE 7.3 Pairing Routine for Unilateral Lower-Body Exercises

Exercise	Reps	Resistance	Between-set rest break
Side lunge	4-6	65%-85% 1RM	30 s-4 min
Front lunge	4-6	65%-85% 1RM	30 s-4 min
Side lunge	4-6	65%-85% 1RM	30 s-4 min
Front lunge	4-6	65%-85% 1RM	30 s-4 min
Side lunge	4-6	65%-85% 1RM	30 s-4 min
Front lunge	4-6	65%-85% 1RM	30 s-4 min

TABLE 7.4   Pairing Routine for Upper-Body Exercises

Exercise	Reps	Resistance	Between-set rest break
Shoulder press	4-6	65%-85% 1RM	30 s-4 min
Dip	4-6	65%-85% 1RM	30 s-4 min
Shoulder press	4-6	65%-85% 1RM	30 s-4 min
Dip	4-6	65%-85% 1RM	30 s-4 min
Shoulder press	4-6	65%-85% 1RM	30 s-4 min
Dip	4-6	65%-85% 1RM	30 s-4 min

TABLE 7.5 Pairing Routine for Lower-Body Exercises with Upper-Body Exercises

Exercise	Reps	Resistance	Between-set rest break
Back squat	4-6	65%-85% 1RM	30 s-4 min
Lateral cable raise	4-6	65%-85% 1RM	30 s-4 min
Back squat	4-6	65%-85% 1RM	30 s-4 min
Lateral cable raise	4-6	65%-85% 1RM	30 s-4 min
Back squat	4-6	65%-85% 1RM	30 s-4 min
Lateral cable raise	4-6	65%-85% 1RM	30 s-4 min

TABLE 7.6   Pairing Routine for Agonist–Antagonist Exercises

Exercise	Reps	Resistance	Between-set rest break
Hip abduction	4-6	65%-85% 1RM	30 s-4 min
Hip adduction	4-6	65%-85% 1RM	30 s-4 min
Hip abduction	4-6	65%-85% 1RM	30 s-4 min
Hip adduction	4-6	65%-85% 1RM	30 s-4 min
Hip abduction	4-6	65%-85% 1RM	30 s-4 min
Hip adduction	4-6	65%-85% 1RM	30 s-4 min

TABLE 7.7   Pairing Routine for Multijoint Exercises with Single-Joint Exercises

Exercise	Reps	Resistance	Between-set rest break
Power shrug	4-6	65%-85% 1RM	30 s-4 min
Shoulder shrug	4-6	65%-85% 1RM	30 s-4 min
Power shrug	4-6	65%-85% 1RM	30 s-4 min
Shoulder shrug	4-6	65%-85% 1RM	30 s-4 min
Power shrug	4-6	65%-85% 1RM	30 s-4 min
Shoulder shrug	4-6	65%-85% 1RM	30 s-4 min

Sample Workouts

Table 7.8 shows a sample workout in which the primary goal is muscle strength improvement. Table 7.9 shows a sample workout in which the primary goal is increased muscle mass.

TABLE 7.8   Sample Workout: Primary Goal Is Muscle Strength Improvement

Exercise	Reps	Resistance	Intraset rest break
Modified Romanian deadlift	4-6	≥80% 1RM	1 min
Back squat	4-6	≥80% 1RM	1 min
Modified Romanian deadlift	4-6	≥80% 1RM	1 min
Back squat	4-6	≥80% 1RM	1 min
Modified Romanian deadlift	4-6	≥80% 1RM	1 min
Back squat	4-6	≥80% 1RM	1 min

TABLE 7.9   Sample Workout: Primary Goal Is Increased Muscle Mass

Exercise	Reps	Resistance	Intraset rest break
Traditional deadlift	4-6	≥80% 1RM	2 min
Prone knee flexion	4-6	≥80% 1RM	2 min
Traditional deadlift	4-6	≥80% 1RM	2 min
Prone knee flexion	4-6	≥80% 1RM	2 min
Traditional deadlift	4-6	≥80% 1RM	2 min
Prone knee flexion	4-6	≥80% 1RM	2 min
Traditional deadlift	4-6	≥80% 1RM	2 min
Prone knee flexion	4-6	≥80% 1RM	2 min
Traditional deadlift	4-6	≥80% 1RM	2 min
Prone knee flexion	4-6	≥80% 1RM	2 min

Conclusion

Muscle clocks need a regularly scheduled exercise program to establish rhythms and initiate the physiological changes associated with muscle strength. One way to do that is to use biomechanically similar paired exercises to provide critical cues about exercise mode. However, other timing cues, such as training intensity and volume, are equally important.

8 | Using Muscle Clocks to Train for Power

Paired exercise training is an effective training method used to develop muscle power. This chapter provides a detailed account of how to use biomechanically similar exercises to program for muscle power outcomes. It demonstrates how to build single-session workouts and programs to improve power using complex training as the guide and the paired exercises detailed in chapter 4. This chapter also explores the science behind complex training concepts, such as neural priming and postactivation potentiation. Paired exercise training relates these concepts to the cues that muscle time clocks seek. Other aspects of the chapter are programming specifics, such as establishing readiness for plyometric exercise training, and suggested intensity and volume guidelines. Sample routines and a programming summary wrap up the chapter for immediate application to training.

Complex Training

Although the focus of this chapter is developing muscle power, it is important to recognize that muscle power is a function of muscle strength, and hence the two muscle outcomes are interdependent and usually combined in training sessions. Combined strength and power training is called *complex training*, which is designed to improve both muscle strength and power.

Because one of the primary goals of complex training is power development, complex training is particularly applicable to sports in which the ability to produce muscle force quickly or execute explosive movements is critical to performance. By using explosive (plyometric) exercises, it is possible to train both muscle strength and power primarily, with a secondary outcome of muscle endurance within the same session. What differentiates complex training from other modes of training is that it

1. uses biomechanically paired exercises and
2. pairs a conditioning exercise (a heavy-load, high-intensity exercise) with an explosive plyometric exercise.

The conditioning exercise can be a multijoint compound exercise or a single-joint isolation exercise.

The term *complex paired workout* defines the unique training method. An example of a complex paired set is a high-load, high-intensity back squat paired with a low-intensity plyometric exercise such as a jump squat (1).

Complex training is an advanced form of strength and power conditioning, suitable for trained exercisers, and relies on the exerciser having

- a solid baseline level of fitness,
- a foundation of muscle strength,
- experience with advanced compound weight training exercises, and
- a motor program (neural blueprint) for common compound exercises.

As mentioned earlier, complex training is most commonly used in athletic training settings. It is common to see it used in American football training rooms in which players have different goals, such as strength or power or a combination of both, based on their position-specific required skills. Exercises are paired and programmed to meet specific training goals and muscle performance outcomes. For example, a lineman would have a different required skill set and training paradigm than a wide receiver.

Programming Template

Complex training is an advanced mode of training most likely to be used by experienced exercisers as a part of a comprehensive program. It is also reasonable to assume that complex paired training is used during individual workouts as part of a comprehensive and lengthy periodization training program. Therefore, the programming template (table 8.1) is an example of an individual paired exercise workout session and should be modified for different athletes and exercisers and workouts and programs.

Postactivation Potentiation

Postactivation potentiation (PAP) is the physiological mechanism that supports the effectiveness of complex training. The method is based on the theory that an exercise done before another similar exercise will make the muscle fibers more responsive for the second exercise. The scientific basis

TABLE 8.1 Programming Template for the Complex Paired Training Method

Exercise	Reps	Resistance	Between-set rest break
Conditioning exercise	4-6	65%-85% 1RM	30 s-4 min
Plyometric exercise	5-8	To be determined*	30 s-4 min
Conditioning exercise	4-6	65%-85% 1RM	30 s-4 min
Plyometric exercise	5-8	To be determined*	30 s-4 min
Conditioning exercise	4-6	65%-85% 1RM	30 s-4 min
Plyometric exercise	5-8	To be determined*	30 s-4 min

* In this context, the personal trainer will determine the appropriateness of using external weight during plyometric exercises. It is uncommon to see external weight used with plyometric exercises; however, for the most advanced exercisers, including athletes, external weight might be used.

is similar to the concept of neural priming, which asserts that if a neural pathway is used over and over, the pathway is reinforced, becomes stronger, and can be easily called on when needed to execute a movement.

The difference between neural priming and PAP is that the former is a nervous system event whereas the latter works in the muscle fibers. Post-activation potentiation uses the first exercise to ready the muscle fibers for the second exercise. The assumption is that the conditioning exercise maximizes the contractility properties of the muscle fibers, readying them for the plyometric exercise, increasing the effectiveness of the explosive exercise in improving muscle power outcomes.

Although PAP and neural priming do differ, PAP relies on neural priming to work efficiently. Neural priming asserts that doing a movement over and over trains the desired neural pathways associated with the desired movements. In that way, priming readies the nerves for quicker action, making it easier to recruit the desired muscle fibers faster and making the nerves and the movement itself more efficient. This is why a solid strength and conditioning foundation is necessary for executing effective complex training. It would not be prudent or effective to try to teach someone a new motor skill, such as an all-body power exercise, at the same time it is being used in a complex training paradigm. Neither the neural pathways nor the muscle fibers are ready to activate the benefits associated with neural priming and PAP, which are required for complex training effectiveness.

Programming for Existing Fitness Level

Complex training is best suited for athletes and elite recreational exercisers who have already achieved a baseline of fitness and strength (1) because

1. basic cardiovascular endurance and muscular endurance, strength, and power are required to execute a high-intensity conditioning exercise and a plyometric exercise back-to-back and
2. the brains and muscles of experienced athletes are more responsive to the priming effects of PAP and the effects of the conditioning exercise on the plyometric exercise.

Programming for Baseline Strength Levels

Before starting a complex training program that includes conditioning exercises plus plyometric exercises, it is essential to make certain that the following baseline levels of muscle strength have been obtained by the athlete (5).

1. For lower-body strength, the athlete or exerciser should be able to squat 1.5 times his or her body weight.
2. For upper-body strength, athletes who weigh >220 lb (>100 kg) need to be able to bench press their body weight. Athletes who weigh <220 lb (<100 kg) need to be able to bench press at least 1.5 times their body weight or perform 5 clap push-ups in a row.

Conditioning Exercise Intensity (Amount of Weight)

The conditioning exercise is the priming exercise; therefore, it must be selected carefully to match the biomechanics of the plyometric exercise that will follow. Along with the muscles used and joint action of the conditioning exercise, the amount of weight used is critical to determining how well it primes the muscles for the second exercise, the plyometric exercise. The amount of weight used during the high-intensity conditioning exercise should be selected on an individual basis and in alignment with current baseline strength levels. In accordance with National Strength and Conditioning Association (NSCA) guidelines and current data on the amount of weight necessary to elicit PAP benefits, the weight used for the conditioning exercise should be 65% to 85% 1RM (5). For muscle strength and power outcomes, the intensity should be closer to the higher end of the range.

Establishing Readiness for Plyometric Exercises

Plyometric exercises are advanced exercises just like all-body power exercises and compound exercises. For that reason, complex training is best suited for athletes and recreational exercisers who have already achieved a baseline of neuromuscular readiness (1). The neuromuscular systems of experienced exercisers are trained, and their muscles are conditioned and more likely to be responsive to the priming effects of the conditioning exercise (heavy-load, high-intensity exercise) on the plyometric exercise. An inexperienced exerciser will not have the motor program (neural blueprint) for most compound and plyometric exercises and thus will not benefit from the priming effect of the conditioning exercise on the plyometric exercise.

General guidelines suggest that before starting a plyometric program with any athlete, make certain the following baseline levels of muscle speed have been obtained (5).

1. For lower-body speed, athletes should be able to complete 5 repetitions of the back squat at 60% or more of their body weight in 5 s or less.
2. For upper-body speed, athletes should be able to complete 5 repetitions of the bench press at 60% or more of their body weight in 5 s or less.

It is important to remember that these guidelines are suggested starting places and not all athletes or exercisers will fall perfectly into each readiness category. Discretion is recommended by each professional based on each athlete's unique abilities and characteristics.

Deconditioned Athletes and Recreational Exercisers

In accordance with inexperienced exercisers, deconditioned athletes and recreational exercisers who have not trained for a while will also not benefit from PAP. It is important to note that although complex training has been shown to be effective for athletes and highly trained recreational exercisers, it has not been shown to have an advantage over conventional training methods for detrained and deconditioned novice exercisers (3). Just as muscles begin to lose endurance, size, strength, and power within 96 h of the last training session (1), neuromuscular adaptations and motor programs are lost over time too. Therefore, caution is urged when considering the utility of high-intensity complex paired training workouts when retraining or returning to strength and conditioning workouts, even with previously experienced exercisers.

Complex Exercise Pairing

Once a practitioner has decided that complex training is an appropriate mode of training for an athlete or exerciser, the next step is exercise selection. Deciding which exercises pair best together is the most important aspect of designing an effective complex paired workout session and entirely depends on individual goals, fitness level, limitations, and preferences.

The first step to effectively pairing conditioning and plyometric exercises is to determine the training goal associated with the use of the complex paired training and the rationale for using such to achieve the goal. Typical intended outcomes of paired complex training include

- strength training,
- power training,
- sport-specific movement training, and
- advanced functional training.

Once a goal and rationale have been developed, the second step is to select specific exercises that will achieve the desired training outcome. Note that the selected paired exercises should use similar movement patterns but be different enough to vary the patterns of muscle activation. For example, pairing a standard split squat with a split jump squat achieves both goals for sport-specific movement training. The movements are biomechanically similar, while the jumping action of the split squat recruits additional muscle fibers to the standard split squat.

Another example is the difference between using a multijoint conditioning exercise versus a single-joint conditioning exercise. For instance, a single-joint movement may be an effective way to improve body composition, but if overall strength is the intended outcome, a multijoint movement is a better choice (4).

Same or Similar Muscles Used

Biomechanically similar exercises work the same or similar muscles. However, the goal of a paired exercise training model is to activate the same muscles or muscle groups in two different ways for both strength (heavy-load, high-intensity exercise) and power (plyometric exercise). Different movement patterns use different bundles of muscle fibers within the same muscle, while different intensities and speeds train both strength and power outcomes. For example, both a back squat (figure 8.1) and jump squat (figure 8.2) train the muscles of the legs and hips. However, to achieve the jump, the jump squat exercise activates more bundles of muscle fibers within the same muscles than the regular squat. The end programming result is a more comprehensive workout for the entire muscle group, training both strength and power in alignment with the intended complex training outcomes.

Same or Similar Joint Actions Used

Pairing a conditioning exercise with a plyometric exercise that uses similar joint actions establishes biomechanical similarity. For example, the paired exercises can use similar joint actions such as shoulder abduction and adduction used during a dumbbell fly (figure 8.3) with shoulder horizontal adduction and horizontal abduction and shoulder girdle abduction and adduction with the plyometric push-up (figure 8.4). Adding a plyometric exercise that uses the same joint actions increases the muscle fiber recruitment and adds a speed training aspect to the workout.

FIGURE 8.1   Back squat: (*a*) starting position; (*b*) bottom position.

FIGURE 8.2   Jump squat: (*a*) position after countermovement; (*b*) highest position.

FIGURE 8.3   Dumbbell fly: (*a*) starting position; (*b*) bottom position.

FIGURE 8.4   Plyometric push-up: (*a*) position after countermovement; (*b*) highest position.

Timing Cues

Muscles learn exercise-specific timing cues from training. Cues are delivered based on the primary muscles trained and the joint actions performed during each exercise when exercises are performed at specific times of the day. For example, a triceps pushdown is similar to a triceps overhead press because both exercises use the triceps muscles as the primary muscle and elbow flexion and extension as the primary joint action. With a regularly scheduled exercise program, the similarity of movement between the two triceps exercises provides muscle clocks with cues about the training mode and type(s) of exercises to anticipate in an upcoming training session and when.

Power exercises are different from strength exercises. Relying on speed, power exercises use plyometric drills that incorporate quicker movements and rely on muscle's ability to generate force after stretching. Because stretch is a primary stimulus for muscle growth, plyometric exercises that deliver timing cues about when stretch will occur and with what exercises provide muscle clocks an unique advantage to prepare for upcoming training sessions to improve muscle performance. Complex training, pairing a strength exercise with an explosive plyometric exercise, adds a new timing cue based on PAP and muscle contractility.

Use of Biomechanically Similar Exercises

Complex training starts with pairing two biomechanically similar exercises, a conditioning exercise plus a plyometric exercise that uses similar muscles and muscle groups and joint actions. For example, the power clean and vertical jump are biomechanically paired exercises that can be used to develop complex paired training sessions. In this case, the conditioning exercise is the power clean (figure 8.5) and the vertical jump (figure 8.6) is the plyometric exercise.

FIGURE 8.5 Power clean: (a) starting position; (b) transition; (c) catch.

FIGURE 8.6 Vertical jump: (*a*) position after countermovement; (*b*) highest position.

Testosterone Levels

It is well established that testosterone levels naturally fluctuate throughout the day. Muscle clocks are aware of these fluctuations and account for them when setting and resetting 24 h biological rhythms. Testosterone levels are highest in the morning and then begin to level off between 4 and 6 p.m., decreasing after that. The daily fluctuation in testosterone levels is a perfect example of synchrony within the human body; natural-occurring levels of a hormone required for muscle strength and power are highest early in the day when internal clocks anticipate activity and decrease ahead of anticipated rest.

Although testosterone levels change throughout the day at times consistent with activity and rest in most people, testosterone levels can be manipulated by other factors, such as resistance training. Resistance training influences testosterone levels both during and after a resistance training session (6). Multijoint exercises, such as the squat and deadlift, are recognized as the most effective way to stimulate the release of testosterone. However, high-intensity exercises in general, such as those used to develop muscle power (for example, a jump squat), can be beneficial as well. Although a jump squat will not use as much external weight as a regular squat, it will stimulate the release of testosterone.

More specific than resistance training only, testosterone levels respond differently to different exercises, such as the deadlift versus the dumbbell curl. For example, a plyometric Smith bench press (figure 8.7), an upper-body exercise and stressor, releases more testosterone into the bloodstream than a seated machine triceps pushdown exercise (figure 8.8), a single-joint exercise using one joint (elbow) and one muscle group (triceps). The difference in the amount of testosterone released is related to the volume of muscle mass used and the overall intensity differences between the two types of exercises: A plyometric Smith bench press uses a large muscle in the body (the pectoralis major), and the seated machine triceps pushdown exercise uses a small one (the triceps). Clearly, the plyometric Smith bench press exercise is more intense than the seated machine triceps pushdown exercise and would be a more effective exercise for releasing testosterone and human growth hormone (HGH). Therefore, it can be argued that the plyometric Smith bench press is a better cue for muscle clocks than the seated machine triceps pushdown, although they are biomechanically similar in that they both use elbow extension to complete the exercises.

Human Growth Hormone Release

HGH is released into the blood during resistance training. High-intensity, compound, multijoint exercises, such as the jump squat, that are used to train muscle power are effective in promoting that release (2). The release

FIGURE 8.7 Plyometric Smith bench press: (*a*) position after countermovement; (*b*) ending (released) position.

FIGURE 8.8   Seated machine triceps pushdown : (*a*) start (highest) position; (*b*) end (lowest) position.

of HGH during power training is an invaluable cue to muscle clocks about the time of day and the type of exercises to expect and when.

Cortisol Release

Resistance training is a source of stress; therefore, it causes the unavoidable release of cortisol into the bloodstream. Although cortisol is largely perceived as a negative hormone associated with negative outcomes (such as an increase in fat mass), repeated bouts of exercise lead to lower levels of cortisol over time.

Like most of the body's chemicals, it has been established that cortisol also has its own natural daily rhythm. Natural cortisol levels are at their highest around 8 a.m. and lowest at 3 to 4 a.m., a pattern similar to testosterone and one that indicates a greater need for cortisol while awake and alert than while resting and sleeping. Similar to other biochemical markers in the body, such as testosterone and HGH, cortisol levels fluctuate throughout the day but also increase or decrease in response to their environment, such as exercise and training demands.

Training for muscle power relies on quick, high-intensity, all-body power exercises that are known to increase cortisol levels and can serve as a valuable timing cue for muscle clocks to anticipate upcoming exercise sessions.

Cortisol release would be similar between two large compound exercises, such as the jump squat and plyometric Smith bench press, but would be less for a single-joint exercise, such as a machine seated knee extension or prone lying leg curl.

Complex Training Programming

At the heart of complex training is superset training. By design, complex training is superset training or performing two exercises back to back with a brief rest period between each exercise set. Remember that rest intervals between exercises and sets are inversely related to intensity: The higher the intensity of an exercise, the more time should be allowed for rest.

In a complex paired training model, the first exercise is a strength exercise with a heavy external weight, termed the *conditioning exercise*, while the second exercise is a lower-resistance plyometric exercise, which is categorized as low, medium, or high based on the level of difficulty.

In traditional complex training, the conditioning exercise is a multijoint all-body power exercise. However, single-joint isolation exercises may be substituted for all-body power exercises. Whether an all-body power movement instead of an isolation exercise is used depends on the exerciser's goals and can vary with each individual workout. A typical paired training set uses 4 to 6 repetitions of the conditioning exercise followed by 5 to 8 repetitions of the plyometric exercise.

In congruence with all concurrent training recommendations, a rest period of 48 h after complex training is required for a complete return to baseline strength. Any rest period beyond 96 h, however, has been shown to result in detraining (1) and should be avoided.

Using Mode (Type of Exercise) to Design Workouts

Consistent with an exercise training and programming method that focuses on biomechanically similar paired exercises, the mode or type of exercise is the most important programming variable. With complex training, the mode is always resistance training and the variation occurs only between the heavy-load, high-intensity conditioning exercise and the second exercise in the superset, which is the explosive training plyometric exercise.

Other mode issues related to complex training include multi- or single-joint exercises, unilateral or bilateral exercises, and the intensity of the plyometric exercise. As with all modes of exercise discussed in this book, pairing exercises with similar muscle and joint actions is the unique programming variable that provides muscle clocks consistent cues about upcoming exercise sessions.

Lower-Body Exercises

Lower-body exercises use the muscles and joints of only the lower body in the performance of the exercise. Lower-body exercises include compound exercises such as squats and leg presses that use large muscles and muscle groups. These exercises maximize testosterone and HGH release and have a proven role in increasing muscle size and improving strength and power. In complex training, lower-body exercises are used most frequently as the conditioning exercise (first exercise) in the paired set.

A study compared the effects of a complex training program and a conventional training program on power and strength development in lower-body muscles (3). A total of 16 participants were assigned to either a complex training group or a conventional training group, both of which completed a resistance training program of similar volume and intensity. The complex training group performed maximum strength exercises with power exercises. For the first 4 weeks, the conventional training group performed exercises similar to the complex training group, then performed equivalent power training during the second half of the program. Both programs produced gains in the weight lifted for the 1RM back squat and the jump squat. The complex training group achieved gains in maximum strength, countermovement jump height, and 10, 15, and 20 m (33, 49, 65.6 ft) runs, while the conventional training group achieved improvements in the 5 m (16.4 ft) run. The results of this study indicate that complex training is more effective than conventional training to develop both strength and power for long endurance events. However, traditional training is best suited, at least as shown by this study, to preferentially affect very short duration running performance.

Upper-Body Exercises

Upper-body exercises use only the muscles and joints of the upper body in exercise performance. Upper-body exercises such as the bench press may include large movements and are known to increase testosterone and HGH levels similar to lower-body compound movements. Although it is possible for a compound exercise such as a bench press to be used as the conditioning or first exercise in a complex paired set, it is less common than a squat, for example.

Unilateral Exercises

Unilateral lower-body exercises use only one side of the body to complete the movement while the opposite side of the body helps support and stabilize the exerciser. Unilateral exercises can use small muscles, such as those of the upper arm in a biceps curl, but they can also use larger muscles, such as those in the leg during a single-leg squat. Unilateral exercises are particularly relevant to sport training when performance is focused on one arm (for example, for a javelin throw). However, unilateral exercises are more likely to be used to train each side of the body equally.

Bilateral Exercises

Bilateral lower-body exercises use and stress both sides of the body. Ideally, each side of the body is worked equally during a bilateral exercise. Bilateral exercises can be single- or multijoint exercises and can even include single-muscle group exercises, such as prone knee flexion for the hamstrings, or many muscle exercises, such as deadlifts.

Agonist–Antagonist Exercises

Agonist–antagonist or functional opposite muscle set training is common in all training settings. It speeds up workout times and is great for overall conditioning. Agonist–antagonist training relies on working one muscle (*agonist*) while the opposite muscle (*antagonist*) lengthens or relaxes and vice versa. This is reciprocal inhibition in action. The bottom line is paired agonist–antagonists sets keep the targeted muscles active during each set.

Agonist–antagonist training is arguably *not* complex training because the two exercises are not biomechanically similar. However, they are included here because the method is popular and has been compared and contrasted with traditional complex training for strength and power outcomes.

A commonly studied pairing is a bench press followed by a pull exercise such as a row. The research question is, Does agonist–antagonist complex pairings (one exercise is a plyometric drill) affect power development similar to traditional complex training? In brief, the answer is that when agonist–antagonist paired training has been used in complex training (plyometric) settings it has been shown to be effective for strength development but not necessarily for power development (1).

Intensity

The principle of individuality is paramount to programming complex training workouts for both safety and effectiveness. The amount of weight used during the conditioning exercise should be selected on an individual basis and in alignment with current baseline strength levels. In accordance with NSCA guidelines and current data on the amount of weight necessary to elicit PAP benefits, the weight used for the conditioning exercise should be 65% to 85% 1RM (5).

Volume

Along with frequency, the volume or amount of training makes up half of the total training load and is reflected over each workout and weekly to monthly. In resistance training, the volume is the total number of repetitions and sets completed within one session and then combined with the frequency to reflect the total amount of work done over a week or longer. Complex training used to develop muscle power is a high-intensity mode of training; therefore, total volume should be kept low to minimize training load and ensure adequate recovery time. Because frequency of training over 24 h periods is a vital timing cue that muscles are looking for, it is important to manipulate volume versus frequency to maintain consistent cues.

Work–Rest Periods

Throughout this book, it has been well documented that muscle clocks rely on regularly scheduled work–rest periods for vital timing cues. These work–rest cycles provide muscle clocks a unique way to determine what to anticipate each 24 h period. The intensity of exercise as well as when it occurs is very helpful to muscle clocks for learning a regular work–rest cycle. High-intensity exercises like those used during complex training are clear signals to muscle clocks that activity is occurring and when it is occurring during a 24 h period.

The most important aspect of complex training is the relationship between the first and second sets. Remember that the first set (conditioning exercise) is priming the muscles to be better at the second set (plyometric exercise). The efficacy of the training method relies on the first set to excite the muscle and enhance contractility. Too much rest between sets and the muscle resets, limiting the effectiveness of the first set on the second set. Too much rest between sets can cause the priming benefits to be lost.

Many factors contribute to determining the best between-set rest periods. A review of the literature suggests that when high-intensity conditioning exercises are used, 30 s up to 4 min works, with 4 min rests considered optimal for conditioned men and women (1).

Work–rest intervals between sets are important, but, as discussed in chapter 7, rest within sets is an important programming variable as well. In regard to power training, one study compared the effects of traditional sets against two different cluster set structures (one group did two cluster sets while the other did four cluster sets) (7). The difference between a traditional set and a cluster set is that a cluster set includes within-set rest periods.

Researchers compared the two training methods on the effects on muscle force, velocity, and power during back squats in men who had strength training experience. Each group of participants performed 3 sets of 12 repetitions at 60% 1RM.

The results showed that when averaged across all repetitions, peak velocity, mean velocity, peak power, and mean power were greater in cluster sets of two and four than in the traditional sets. These results suggest that within-set rest breaks are more effective for training power than traditional sets with between-set rest periods.

Another important finding was that when individual sets within each training group were compared, peak velocity, mean velocity, peak power, and mean power decreased during the course of traditional sets whereas no decreases were noted during cluster sets. In other words, within-set breaks allow muscles to work harder and faster during the entire set versus traditional sets. These findings show that cluster set structures maintain velocity and power whereas traditional set structures do not. For power training, increasing the frequency of within-set rest intervals in cluster set training maximizes this effect and is recommended if maximal velocity is to be sustained during training.

Resistance and Plyometric Exercise Pairing Routines

By using plyometric exercises, it is possible to train muscle strength and power primarily, with a secondary focus on muscle endurance within the same session. What differentiates complex training from other modes of training is that it

1. uses biomechanically paired exercises, and
2. pairs a biomechanically similar conditioning exercise (heavy-load, high-intensity exercise) with a plyometric exercise.

The remainder of this chapter is devoted to showing potential exercise pairings and complex training method paradigms. Table 8.2 through table 8.11 do not cover all possible pairings; rather, they are meant to illustrate the most common ways to pair exercises.

TABLE 8.2 Unilateral Lower-Body Exercise with Low-Intensity Plyometric Exercise

Exercise	Reps	Resistance	Between-set rest break
Step-up	4-6	65%-85% 1RM	30 s-4 min
Single-leg pushoff	5-8	Body weight	30 s-4 min
Step-up	4-6	65%-85% 1RM	30 s-4 min
Single-leg pushoff	5-8	Body weight	30 s-4 min
Step-up	4-6	65%-85% 1RM	30 s-4 min
Single-leg pushoff	5-8	Body weight	30 s-4 min

TABLE 8.3 Unilateral Lower-Body Exercise with Medium-Intensity Plyometric Exercise

Exercise	Reps	Resistance	Between-set rest break
Split squat	4-6	65%-85% 1RM	30 s-4 min
Single-arm alternate leg bound	5-8	Body weight	30 s-4 min
Split squat	4-6	65%-85% 1RM	30 s-4 min
Single-arm alternate leg bound	5-8	Body weight	30 s-4 min
Split squat	4-6	65%-85% 1RM	30 s-4 min
Single-arm alternate leg bound	5-8	Body weight	30 s-4 min

TABLE 8.4 Unilateral Lower-Body Exercise with High-Intensity Plyometric Exercise

Exercise	Reps	Resistance	Between-set rest break
Lunge	4-6	65%-85% 1RM	30 s-4 min
Depth jump to second box	5-8	Body weight	30 s-4 min
Lunge	4-6	65%-85% 1RM	30 s-4 min
Depth jump to second box	5-8	Body weight	30 s-4 min
Lunge	4-6	65%-85% 1RM	30 s-4 min
Depth jump to second box	5-8	Body weight	30 s-4 min

TABLE 8.5 Bilateral Lower-Body Exercise with Low-Intensity Plyometric Exercise

Exercise	Reps	Resistance	Between-set rest break
Front squat	4-6	65%-85% 1RM	30 s-4 min
Jump and reach	5-8	Body weight	30 s-4 min
Front squat	4-6	65%-85% 1RM	30 s-4 min
Jump and reach	5-8	Body weight	30 s-4 min
Front squat	4-6	65%-85% 1RM	30 s-4 min
Jump and reach	5-8	Body weight	30 s-4 min

TABLE 8.6 Bilateral Lower-Body Exercise with Medium-Intensity Plyometric Exercise

Exercise	Reps	Resistance	Between-set rest break
Leg press	4-6	65%-85% 1RM	30 s-4 min
Lateral box jump	5-8	Body weight	30 s-4 min
Leg press	4-6	65%-85% 1RM	30 s-4 min
Lateral box jump	5-8	Body weight	30 s-4 min
Leg press	4-6	65%-85% 1RM	30 s-4 min
Lateral box jump	5-8	Body weight	30 s-4 min

TABLE 8.7 Bilateral Lower-Body Exercise with High-Intensity Plyometric Exercise

Exercise	Reps	Resistance	Between-set rest break
Back squat	4-6	65%-85% 1RM	30 s-4 min
Pike jump	5-8	Body weight	30 s-4 min
Back squat	4-6	65%-85% 1RM	30 s-4 min
Pike jump	5-8	Body weight	30 s-4 min
Back squat	4-6	65%-85% 1RM	30 s-4 min
Pike jump	5-8	Body weight	30 s-4 min

TABLE 8.8 Upper-Body Exercise with Low-Intensity Plyometric Exercise

Exercise	Reps	Resistance	Between-set rest break
Weighted push-up	4-6	65%-85% 1RM	30 s-4 min
Medicine ball chest pass	5-8	To be determined*	30 s-4 min
Weighted push-up	4-6	65%-85% 1RM	30 s-4 min
Medicine ball chest pass	5-8	To be determined*	30 s-4 min
Weighted push-up	4-6	65%-85% 1RM	30 s-4 min
Medicine ball chest pass	5-8	To be determined*	30 s-4 min

* The general rule when determining the weight of the medicine ball is the ball must be heavy enough to slow the exercise but not so heavy to reduce range of motion or make it difficult for the athlete to comfortably control the ball for at least 5 repetitions.

TABLE 8.9 Upper-Body Exercise with Medium-Intensity Plyometric Exercise

Exercise	Reps	Resistance	Between-set rest break
Dumbbell bench press	4-6	65%-85% 1RM	30 s-4 min
Plyometric or clap push-up	5-8	Body weight	30 s-4 min
Dumbbell bench press	4-6	65%-85% 1RM	30 s-4 min
Plyometric or clap push-up	5-8	Body weight	30 s-4 min
Dumbbell bench press	4-6	65%-85% 1RM	30 s-4 min
Plyometric or clap push-up	5-8	Body weight	30 s-4 min

TABLE 8.10 Upper-Body Exercise with High-Intensity Plyometric Exercise

Exercise	Reps	Resistance	Between-set rest break
Barbell bench press	4-6	65%-85% 1RM	30 s-4 min
Explosive bench press throw on Smith machine	5-8	Bar weight	30 s-4 min
Barbell bench press	4-6	65%-85% 1RM	30 s-4 min
Explosive bench press throw on Smith machine	5-8	Bar weight	30 s-4 min
Barbell bench press	4-6	65%-85% 1RM	30 s-4 min
Explosive bench press throw on Smith machine	5-8	Bar weight	30 s-4 min

TABLE 8.11   Agonist–Antagonist Exercise Pairing

Exercise	Reps	Resistance	Between-set rest break
Bent-over row	4-6	65%-85% 1RM	30 s-4 min
Plyometric push-up	5-8	Body weight	30 s-4 min
Bent-over row	4-6	65%-85% 1RM	30 s-4 min
Plyometric push-up	5-8	Body weight	30 s-4 min
Bent-over row	4-6	65%-85% 1RM	30 s-4 min
Plyometric push-up	5-8	Body weight	30 s-4 min

Sample Workouts

Table 8.12 shows a sample workout in which the primary goal is power improvement. Table 8.13 shows a sample workout in which the primary goal is body composition change.

TABLE 8.12 Sample Workout: Primary Goal Is Power Improvement

Exercise	Reps	Cluster sets	Resistance	Within-set rest break
All-body power exercise	4-32	1-2	65%-85% 1RM	30 s
High-intensity plyometric exercise	4-32	1-2	Body weight	30 s

TABLE 8.13 Sample Workout: Primary Goal Is Body Composition Change

Exercise	Reps	Resistance	Between-set rest break
Unilateral or bilateral lower-body exercise	4-6	65%-85% 1RM	30 s-4 min
Low- to high-intensity plyometric exercise	5-8	To be determined*	30 s-4 min
Unilateral or bilateral lower-body exercise	4-6	65%-85% 1RM	30 s-4 min
Low- to high-intensity plyometric exercise	5-8	To be determined*	30 s-4 min
Unilateral or bilateral lower-body exercise	4-6	65%-85% 1RM	30 s-4 min
Low- to high-intensity plyometric exercise	5-8	To be determined*	30 s-4 min

* The general rule when determining the resistance to add to a plyometric exercise is the athlete must first be able to execute easily at least 5 repetitions of the exercise using the correct form without weight. Weight should be added sparingly from what is considered a very light load and progressed accordingly for each athlete. Once weight is added, the athlete must be able to execute the plyometric drill with weight using the same mechanics and range of motion as the unweighted version for at least 5 repetitions.

Conclusion

Although complex training is most widely recognized as a way to develop muscle explosiveness, particularly in athletic training settings with well-trained individuals, it is designed to improve both muscle strength and power. To achieve both goals of strength and power development, the complex training method pairs a high-intensity resistance exercise with a biomechanically similar plyometric exercise.

Using paired exercises, complex training delivers important cues to muscle clocks about the timing and intensity of resistance training sessions. Complex training workouts can vary widely from pairing agonist–antagonist muscle groups to pairing unilateral and bilateral exercises and even using an upper-body exercise paired with a lower-body exercise strategy. Regardless of how exercises are paired, complex training relies on key aspects of nervous system control, including neural priming and postactivation potentiation. Together, neural priming and PAP ready the nerves and muscles for quicker action, making it easier for the brain to recruit the desired muscle fibers, execute the exercises, and improve performance.

9 | Using Muscle Clocks for Concurrent Training

Most athletes do concurrent training—combining cardiovascular endurance and resistance training in the same session—because it seems to achieve multiple goals within the same workout. But does it really achieve multiple goals, or is it counterproductive? At this point, it is clear that concurrent training is counterproductive for specific muscle performance goals, although it can have use for general fitness. In regard to muscle performance, concurrent training is counterproductive to developing muscle strength and power if both cardiovascular endurance and muscle strength and power are trained within the same session or too close together within the same day.

Concurrent Training

Concurrent training is doing cardiovascular endurance and resistance training within the same session or closely together within the same day. Long ago in the exercise science world, concurrent training was promoted as a way to save time while reaching multiple training goals. However, it is now clear that the mechanisms of cardiovascular endurance training and resistance training complete with one another at the molecular level and, under certain situations, can cancel each other out, thereby essentially rendering significant muscle strength and power outcomes nonexistent. In fact, the original landmark study on concurrent training outcomes (12) showed that muscle strength actually *decreased* during the last 2 weeks of a concurrent training study period in which the subjects did both cardiovascular endurance and resistance training. These results were significant because they showed that cardiovascular training ceased upper-end strength improvements while leaving cardiovascular endurance, as measured by $\dot{V}O_2$max, unaffected. Since 1980, the message has been that cardiovascular endurance training interferes with muscle strength performance and that the body tends to favor cardiovascular endurance outcomes over muscle strength outcomes.

Concurrent training causes muscle confusion at the molecular level. Consider this: Muscles get confused just like you do. If you walk into a spin center ready for a spin class only to find Pilates equipment on the floor, you get confused. Muscles are the same way. When two competing kinds of exercise, such as cardiovascular endurance training and resistance training, are performed during the same workout session, the involved muscles become confused. Muscle confusion occurs at a molecular level; the molecular mechanisms associated with cardiovascular endurance and muscle strength and power are different. When the two modes of training occur too close in time, muscles simply don't know what to do. In the end, the molecular mechanisms associated with muscle strength and power performance are sacrificed at the expense of cardiovascular endurance goals, and results are diminished.

In one study on concurrent training using contemporary popular training methods (8), researchers studied a combination of high-intensity interval cycling endurance training and high-velocity (or speed) resistance training. The results showed that cycling $\dot{V}O_2$max increased to the same extent in both the endurance training only group and the combined endurance and resistance training group when measured several times over the 7-week period, but strength improvements were different in each group. The resistance training only group had increases in maximal *torque* (the rotary component of force output) whereas the endurance with resistance training group had a significant improvement only at specific torques, suggesting that the interference in strength and power development occurred at high- but not low-velocity rates of force production.

Additional evidence suggests concurrent cardiovascular endurance training interferes with increases in muscle size (15) and thus interferes with strength development. Researchers found that combining cardiovascular endurance and resistance training negatively affected fiber cross-sectional areas. However, in this particular study the authors found that concurrent training compromised strength development only when both modes of exercise engaged the same muscle group, suggesting a local effect rather than a systemic one.

Subsequent studies show something different about local versus systematic effects of concurrent training. One study examined the effects of lower-body sprint interval training on upper-body hypertrophy and strength (14). The results showed that sprint interval training combined with resistance training adversely affected upper-body hypertrophy and strength. This finding is significant because it is counter to earlier research suggesting a local effect of concurrent training. The study showed that the effects of concurrent aerobic endurance and resistance training are not muscle-use specific. Lower-body sprint interval training adversely affected upper-body strength performance; therefore, the effects of endurance training affect nonworking muscles. This is significant in concurrent programming in which most modes of cardiovascular endurance training use the lower body. It appears based on this study that the upper-body muscles are not spared the negative consequences of concurrent training and interference, even when not used. The results suggest that the mechanisms responsible for interference cannot be avoided by working different muscle groups during cardiovascular endurance and resistance training.

Competing Mechanisms

Chapter 2 looked at the competing mechanisms responsible for muscle confusion in detail. Here the mechanisms are expanded to also include neural and substrate factors.

As mentioned in chapter 2, it is critical to have an understanding of muscle confusion before discussing the proposed mechanisms. Muscle force generation capacity (MFGC), a way to measure muscle strength, is the most important concept for understanding muscle training. It is a method of determining whether muscles are actually getting stronger. Specifically in regard to concurrent training, MFGC measures if cardiovascular endurance training interferes with muscle performance.

In one study, researchers measured MFGC over a 4-day test period combining high-intensity, lower-body resistance training with cardiovascular endurance training (7). Unfortunately, the results showed that strength was diminished over the test period when resistance training and cardiovascular endurance training were done in the same session, demonstrating interference. The results clearly indicated that the mechanisms that cause muscle growth, strength, and power outcomes and those associated with cardiovascular endurance changes compete and interfere with one another and reduce the quality of resistance training sessions.

Neural Factors

Another study compared the neuromuscular adaptations between same-session combined resistance and cardiovascular endurance training (cycling) with two loading orders and different-day combined training over 24 weeks (9). Researchers divided 56 subjects into three training groups: different-day combined resistance and cardiovascular endurance training 4 to 6 days per week or same-session combined training in which cardiovascular endurance preceded resistance training or vice versa 2 or 3 days per week.

Researchers measured and analyzed dynamic and isometric resistance, muscle activity, voluntary muscle activation, muscle cross-sectional area, and cardiovascular endurance performance. The results showed that all groups showed improved performance on dynamic 1RM and isometric force, muscle cross-sectional area, and maximal power output during cycling. The different-day and resistance training before cardiovascular training groups showed increased voluntary activation during training. In the cardiovascular training before resistance training group, there was no increase in voluntary activation detected after 12 or 24 weeks.

Other results showed that cardiovascular training before resistance training resulted in no improvement in muscle activity in isometric maximal contractions while the resistance before cardiovascular group increased maximum muscle activity after 24 weeks during maximal isometric muscle actions. This is important because it shows increased neural activity in the resistance training before cardiovascular exercise group and no improvements in neural activation for the cardiovascular before resistance training group. Furthermore, neural adaptations showed indications of being compromised when cardiovascular training was performed before resistance training.

Another study examined neuromuscular adaptations in recreational endurance runners during 24 weeks of same-session combined cardiovascular endurance and resistance training compared to cardiovascular endurance training only (22). The frequency of endurance training was similar in the two research groups, four to six times per week. Additional maximal and explosive resistance training was performed in the concurrent training group and always after incremental running sessions that lasted 35 to 45 min at 65% to 85% of heart rate maximum.

The results showed that maximal dynamic leg press strength remained unchanged in the concurrent training group. However, maximum dynamic leg press strength decreased in the running only group at week 24. Isometric leg press and unilateral knee extension force, muscle activity of knee extensors, and voluntary activation remained unchanged in both groups. The changes in muscle cross-section differed between the two groups after 12 and 24 weeks of training, showing that the concurrent trained group gained more muscle mass than the running only group. Most important, resistance training performed after an endurance running session did not lead to increased maximal strength, muscle size, muscle activity, or voluntary activation, indicating that the mechanisms associated with muscle size, strength, and power improvements were adversely affected by concurrent cardiovascular work, especially if that cardiovascular training was done before resistance training.

Another study compared the effects of 24 weeks of morning to evening same-session concurrent resistance and cardiovascular endurance training on neuromuscular and endurance performance (17). A total of 51 men were assigned to the morning or evening training group in which resistance training was done before cardiovascular exercise or vice versa or to a control group. Researchers measured isometric force, voluntary muscle activation, and peak wattage during a maximal cycling test.

The first significant result was that for training time of day, in the morning, no order specific gains were observed in neuromuscular performance. However, things changed when the evening results were analyzed. In the evening, the changes in isometric muscle force and activity were larger in the resistance training before cardiovascular group versus the resistance training after cardiovascular work. The results indicate that the concurrent training program led to greater neuromuscular adaptations when resistance training was performed before cardiovascular exercise and in the evening.

Concurrent training causes interference that negatively affects muscle strength and power outcomes. Although it has been clear for decades that interference occurs, the mechanisms that underlie and cause interference are still under investigation. In chapter 2, the mechanisms associated with muscle confusion and interference were introduced and explained. In this chapter, those same mechanisms are covered along with additional plausible explanations for how and why muscle confusion and interference occur during concurrent training.

Muscle Factors

Muscles change due to long-term exercise training cause adaptations in endurance, size, strength, and power outcomes. Although muscle changes are positive for the most part, they do not always complement one another, and interference or competition between adaptations can occur. In particular, those that cause cardiovascular fitness and muscle endurance improvements negatively affect muscle size, strength, and power outcomes. Local changes at the muscle are responsible for many of those conflicting mechanisms and are discussed here.

Fiber Type Transformation

Changes in muscle fiber composition are a possible reason that cardiovascular endurance training inhibits muscle strength increases during concurrent training programs (3). It is well known that skeletal muscle hypertrophy as a result of strength training occurs to a greater extent in fast-twitch (type II) than in slow-twitch (type I) muscle fibers (2). However, long duration cardiovascular endurance training in rats has been shown to reduce maximal shortening speed of fast-twitch muscle fibers and to change skeletal muscle fibers from fast-twitch to slow-twitch fibers as measured by changes in myosin ATPase (18). These data suggest that a reduction in the number of fast-twitch muscle fibers by cardiovascular endurance training could play a major role in muscle confusion and interference and thus limit muscle size, strength, and power development during concurrent training.

Contractility

Aside from fiber type transformation, which is a more complex and negative long-term adaptation to concurrent training, something as basic and immediate as muscle contractility is affected by concurrent training. Prolonged cardiovascular endurance training, such as cycling, decreases a muscle's ability to contract effectively and quickly during resistance training and thus causes changes that work against muscle size, strength, and power development (6). This observation supports the idea that when resistance training is done after cardiovascular training, muscle size, strength, and power are adversely affected.

It is also important to recognize that although muscle contractility can affect resistance training outcomes immediately, they are mediated by the length of recovery time, the intensity of each mode of exercise, and the frequency and volume of cardiovascular training.

Delayed Onset Muscle Soreness

Delayed-onset muscle soreness (DOMS) is another possible mechanism for muscle-level interference as a result of concurrent training. DOMS is caused by a series of microscopic muscle events, such as small tears in the muscle fibers, that may prevent muscle size, strength, and power developments. One study has shown that when DOMS happens, strength decreases over the same time in beginning exercisers (1). It is important to note that this study focused on beginning exercisers to support the DOMS theory, and resistance-trained athletes are expected to respond differently. However, the theory still holds that any microscopic tears in muscle fibers would adversely affect resistance training efficiency.

Overtraining

Another reason the mechanisms of cardiovascular and resistance training may compete is simply overtraining. Concurrent resistance and cardiovascular endurance training may lead to overtraining, which can account for the inability of the muscle to attain optimal strength performance (3). In general, overtraining is caused by an imbalance between training and recovery (16), defined by either no improvement or a decline in performance. For example, one study on concurrent training study showed that strength declined in the 9th and 10th weeks of concurrent training (12). The argument was made that the decline in strength was specifically due to overtraining because the concurrent training group did 80 min of training, and the volume of training negatively affected strength development. The muscles were too fatigued to produce adequate force for strength improvements.

However, where strength decrements were found during weeks 9 and 10 of the concurrent training program, measures of cardiovascular endurance work showed no negative effects of fatigue on endurance from concurrent training, again suggesting that the effects of concurrent training preferentially affect strength development.

Substrate Factors

In addition to explanations for muscle confusion and interference at the neural and muscle levels, there are substrate issues—such as glycogen depletion; increased protein breakdown; and testosterone, cortisol, and lactate changes—affecting concurrent training results. These physiological processes occur during cardiovascular endurance training, which reduces available substrates, breaks down protein, and causes fluctuations of other biochemicals necessary for optimal muscle function, affecting muscle size, strength, and power developments.

Protein Breakdown

Protein breakdown during prolonged muscle work also causes DOMS and reduces the efficacy of strength training. However, the more obvious dilemma is that protein is needed to build muscle. Therefore, when protein is depleted, hypertrophy, strength, and power performance are adversely affected.

Cardiovascular endurance training has been shown to reduce protein synthesis rates in skeletal muscles during exercise. Although protein depletion is short term, it causes a decrease in protein synthesis for several hours after exercise (2) and thus interrupts muscle's ability to grow. Therefore, when cardiovascular and resistance training are done within the same session, protein synthesis can be disrupted, leading to little or no muscle fiber size change and thus decreasing strength-related performance (15). The bottom line is that when concurrent training is performed several times a week, it may disrupt the protein synthesis mechanisms required for adaptations to resistance training sessions that yield muscle growth.

Glycogen Levels

Repeated bouts of either resistance or cardiovascular endurance exercise or a combination of both close together in time may produce chronically low muscle glycogen levels that can impair future training sessions. Cardiovascular endurance training on consecutive days can decrease resting muscle glycogen levels (4), and glycogen depletion has been shown after resistance training as well (23). During concurrent training, low muscle glycogen levels might impair the intracellular signaling responses to resistance training and yield little to no muscle strength increases (5). The implication is that a concurrent training program that includes daily or twice daily training sessions may impair the responses to resistance exercise and recovery.

Testosterone

Testosterone levels are another potential explanation for muscle confusion and interference caused by concurrent training. When testosterone levels were compared between resistance training only, cardiovascular training only, and concurrent cardiovascular and resistance training, testosterone levels increased in the strength training only group (7). As expected, testosterone levels decreased in both the endurance only and concurrent training groups. This is a very important finding with far-reaching implications for sport and fitness training and programming.

The critical point here is that testosterone levels are directly related to muscle size, strength, and power performances. The greater the testosterone level, the better the muscle performance. Therefore, if concurrent training reduces testosterone levels, it can clearly decrease the effectiveness of resistance training, highlighting the requirement for careful exercise programming design to avoid muscle confusion and interference.

Blood Lactate and Cortisol Levels

In contrast to the study that examined only testosterone levels (7), another study looked at the effects of concurrent training on MFGC and testosterone, cortisol, and lactate blood concentrations in recreational athletes (13). What they found is critically important for understanding the competing mechanisms that occur during concurrent training. When researchers compared the order of concurrent training—resistance training only to resistance training before and after cardiovascular endurance training, they found that *testosterone increased in all three training conditions*, but MFGC was adversely affected when cardiovascular endurance training was done before resistance training, indicating that cardiovascular training interferes with muscle contractility and reduces muscle force output. Additional results showed that blood lactate and cortisol levels were elevated when resistance training was done after cardiovascular endurance training. The bottom line is this: Doing cardiovascular endurance training before resistance training interferes with strength performance gains by elevating blood lactate and cortisol levels and by affecting contractile properties of the working muscles.

Blood lactate and cortisol levels are additional metabolic factors that determine the efficacy (or lack thereof) of concurrent training. Where it is desirable that testosterone levels be high to yield muscle hypertrophy, strength, and power improvements, the opposite is true of blood lactate and cortisol concentrations. For optimal muscle performance during resistance training, blood lactate and cortisol levels should be low or they interfere with muscle growth, strength, and power improvements. Cardiovascular training before strength training also interferes with muscle hypertrophy, strength, and power by elevating blood lactate and cortisol levels, which interfere with the molecular adaptations associated with the desired performance outcomes.

Molecular Signaling Factors

Long-term resistance training causes muscle hypertrophy by activating a protein-specific growth-facilitation signaling network. However, cardiovascular endurance exercise can negatively affect the protein-signaling network inside muscles, making resistance training less effective for developing muscle mass, strength, and power.

In regard to how muscle growth occurs after resistance training, studies in both humans and rodents have shown that a single resistance training workout causes increased activity of at least three substrates that regulate muscle protein synthesis: phosphoinositide-3-dependent kinase (PI3DK) (11), protein kinase B (PKB) (20), and the ribosomal protein S6 kinase 1 (S6K1) (20). In other words, these proteins build muscles; when they are negatively affected, resistance training will be less effective for building muscle and developing strength and power.

It is well known that cardiovascular endurance training interferes with resistance training outcomes. One of the most plausible explanations as to why this interference occurs is that the molecular signaling mechanisms related to the metabolic adaptations of each type of training (cardiovascular endurance versus resistance training) compete with one another at a cellular level. Most notably, the activation of AMP-activated protein kinase (AMPK), a key factor in regulating cell growth, energy, and homeostasis, is affected by cardiovascular endurance exercise (25). AMPK is regulated by an increase in the ADP/ATP ratio, which occurs naturally during cardiovascular endurance exercise (26). Changes to ADP/ATP and thus AMPK can alter gene expression and reduce substrate availability, which can, in turn, affect cellular adaptations to resistance training during concurrent training (25).

Other substrates negatively influence protein synthesis and are affected by cardiovascular exercise. One substrate in particular, eukaryotic elongation factor 2 (eEF2), was shown to increase immediately during cycling exercise (21). This is very important because an increase in eEF2 inhibits protein synthesis and thus deters muscle growth, strength, and power development from resistance training. In the study, subjects cycled at about 67% of their $\dot{V}O_2$max up to 90 min. Muscle biopsies were taken from each subject at rest and after 1, 10, 30, 60, and 90 min of cycling. The most startling result of the study was that cycling caused a 5- to 7-fold increase in eEF2 within 1 min of the onset of exercise, and it remained elevated for the entire 90 min of exercise, showing how concurrent cardiovascular endurance exercise can negatively affect resistance training outcomes if they are done within 90 min of one another. The increase in eEF2 during cardiovascular endurance training suggests that concurrent training is not the best mode of training if muscle hypertrophy, strength, and power outcomes are the primary goals.

It is reasonable to assume that activation of AMPK and inhibition of the eEF2 by cardiovascular endurance exercise will negatively affect the responses to resistance exercise by affecting training-induced increases in protein synthesis. Concurrent cardiovascular endurance exercise and resistance training can result in activation of antagonist molecular events or inhibition of protein synthesis. Together or alone, either of these events can decrease the anabolic responses required for muscle growth and strength and power development.

Using Muscle Clocks to Avoid Interference in Programming

Muscles are smart and recognize different training conditions such as mode, frequency, volume, and intensity. However, they crave consistency. They use their internal muscle clocks (discussed in chapter 1), via time cues (discussed in chapter 3), to help them find consistency. Muscle clocks help muscles find cues about the time of day and type of training based on scheduled exercise programming. Muscles look for cues from training conditions to determine how to respond by either clicking on the molecular mechanisms responsible for aerobic endurance or muscle hypertrophy, strength, and power improvements.

By now it is clear that resistance and cardiovascular endurance training muscle outcomes are mediated by different molecular actions. When training is chaotic or poorly designed, muscles get confused. They don't know which molecular actions to activate; they can shut down, diminishing the positive effects of training. In that circumstance, it appears that muscle events associated with hypotrophy, strength, and power outcomes are preferentially adversely affected.

The bad news is that concurrent training does appear to hinder muscle growth, strength, and power outcomes while leaving cardiovascular and muscle endurance outcomes relatively unaffected. However, the good news is that research supports the idea that muscle clocks respond to well-structured, systematic exercise training and programming, resetting in response (27). Resetting of muscle clocks means that muscle clocks and muscles reprogram in response to systematic exercise, making the associated changes with upcoming exercise sessions in advance of training.

The data heavily support the conclusion that cardiovascular exercise interferes with muscle growth, strength, and power outcomes. However, cardiovascular training is a vital part of any sport and fitness conditioning program, and it is common to use concurrent training or some combination of cardiovascular endurance training along with resistance training, even if these two different modes of exercise are done on different days or many hours apart.

Based on what is known about muscles, timing-dependent competing mechanisms occur when cardiovascular exercise and resistance training are done together. On the other hand, what is known about muscle clocks supports the idea that systematic exercise programming strategies can help avoid muscle confusion and interference and lessen the negative effects of cardiovascular training on resistance training outcomes.

Cardiovascular Programming to Improve Resistance Training Outcomes

Cardiovascular exercise interferes with resistance training outcomes. As discussed, poorly designed concurrent training programs appear to hinder muscle growth, strength, and power outcomes; however, a thoughtful and carefully designed exercise program can mitigate these effects.

Strategic exercise programming is vital for combating muscle confusion and interference during concurrent training programs. When designing concurrent training programs, the key to using cardiovascular exercise in a concurrent program while avoiding muscle strength and power deficits lies in how workouts and programs are organized over time. When designing a cardiovascular exercise program in which one programming objective is to avoid muscle strength and power decrements, the trainer should consider the following primary programming factors.

- Mode of cardiovascular exercise (e.g., jogging or cycling)
- Frequency (how often) of cardiovascular exercise
- Length of rest periods and recovery time
- Intensity of cardiovascular exercise
- Volume (duration) of cardiovascular exercise

Mode of Cardiovascular Exercise

The first thing to consider when designing a cardiovascular exercise program as part of a concurrent training program in which muscle strength and power are primary focuses is the mode of cardiovascular exercise. Research shows that running combined with resistance training results in greater strength loss than cycling combined with strength training (24). Consequently, it is recommended to include cycling in concurrent training programs versus jogging or running when muscle hypertrophy, strength, and power are primary training goals.

Furthermore, another study shows that longer-duration cardiovascular endurance training is more adverse than shorter-duration, high-intensity endurance sessions on muscle mass, strength, and power outcomes (10). The concurrent programming recommendation is that high-intensity interval training, not continuous aerobic endurance training, should be used with concurrent programs because training volume seems to affect muscle hypertrophy, strength, and power more than does training intensity.

Frequency of Cardiovascular Exercise

If a training program includes both cardiovascular endurance and resistance training goals, it is best to schedule each mode of exercise on alternate days to avoid muscle confusion and interference and, more important, to provide muscle with adequate recovery time between cardiovascular and resistance training (7). Additional programming suggestions include limiting cardiovascular exercise frequency to fewer than 3 days per week to minimize the negative effects on muscle hypertrophy, strength, and power (24).

Length of Rest Periods and Recovery Time

It is common knowledge that muscles need at least 48 h for baseline strength to recover from a high-intensity resistance training session. At least one study supported the industrywide accepted 48 h rest period for muscles (7). Researchers collected data on knee extensor torque, showing that torque (a rotary component of force) and muscle force generation capacity were compromised up to 2 days after high-intensity strength training on alternating days. The data support the programming recommendation that when resistance training is performed at a high intensity (typically defined as ≥85% 1RM), full recovery requires 48 h.

Muscles need 48 h to return to baseline strength after a high-intensity workout. When looking at the molecular mechanisms responsible for strength and power improvements, muscles need a minimum of 3 h to reset after cardiovascular exercise according to one study (13), whereas another study showed molecular mechanisms need closer to 6 h and up to 24 h to fully reset to avoid interference (19). The conclusion is the same: When cardiovascular training is done too closely in time relative to resistance training, it negatively affects the quality of resistance training and interrupts the development of muscle hypertrophy, strength, and power.

Intensity of Cardiovascular Training

Another important research finding that will influence concurrent programming is that the extent of muscle strength and power impairment is directly related to the intensity of the cardiovascular exercise (7). Specifically, moderate- to high-intensity cardiovascular exercise reduced the effectiveness of resistance training.

Therefore, the programming recommendation is that the intensity of cardiovascular exercise sessions should be decreased to limit the negative effect on muscle hypertrophy, strength, and power. However, practical considerations and training goals will influence the utility of low-intensity cardiovascular training sessions. The reality is that low-intensity cardiovascular training sessions may not negatively affect muscle strength and power, but they might not be useful to reaching overall program goals either. The periodic frequency of moderate- to high-intensity sessions might be warranted, and the decision to use low- to moderate- or higher-intensity cardiovascular exercise should be considered on a case-by-case basis according to programming goals.

Volume of Cardiovascular Exercise

Volume is the amount of work done. It is important because it can influence the molecular mechanisms of muscle confusion and interference from very early on during exercise to long durations (21) and adversely affect muscle hypertrophy, strength, and power outcomes. Therefore, the programming recommendation made is that cardiovascular training sessions last 20 to 30 min to moderate the negative effects of volume on strength gains (24).

Programming Summary Statements

In summary, use the following programming guidelines to design a concurrent training program in which the primary goals are muscle hypertrophy, strength, and power.

- Use cycling instead of running as the cardiovascular training exercise.
- Use high-intensity interval training instead of continuous training.
- Rest for at least 48 h after high-intensity exercise (>85% maximum capacity).
- Provide at least 3 h, preferably 6 h, between competing modes of exercise when performing same-day sessions.
- Schedule cardiovascular and resistance training on alternating days if possible.
- Limit cardiovascular training to three times per week or less.
- Use low-intensity cardiovascular workouts.
- Limit cardiovascular sessions to 20 to 30 min.

Tables 9.1 and 9.2 provide sample concurrent training programs.

TABLE 9.1 Sample Cardiovascular Training Program for Muscle Strength Improvement

Day	Exercise mode	Intensity (% $\dot{V}O_2$max)	Duration
Sunday	Off		
Monday	Cycling with HIIT intervals	40%-75%	20-30 min
Tuesday	Off		
Wednesday	Cycling with HIIT intervals	40%-75%	20-30 min
Thursday	Off		
Friday	Cycling with HIIT intervals	40%-75%	20-30 min
Saturday	Off		

Note: An alternative mode is continuous training. However it has a greater negative effect on muscle strength than high-intensity interval training (HIIT).

TABLE 9.2 Sample Resistance Training Program for Cardiovascular Fitness Improvement

Exercise	Time of day for resistance training	Frequency (alternating days/week)	% 1RM	Volume / (sets × repetitions)	Rest break between each paired exercise
Paired resistance training exercise 1	4-6 p.m.	3	65%-85%	2-3 × 10-15	10-60 s
Paired resistance training exercise 2	4-6 p.m.	3	65%-85%	2-3 × 10-15	10-60 s
Paired resistance training exercise 1	4-6 p.m.	3	65%-85%	2-3 × 10-15	10-60 s
Paired resistance training exercise 2	4-6 p.m.	3	65%-85%	2-3 × 10-15	10-60 s
Paired resistance training exercise 1	4-6 p.m.	3	65%-85%	2-3 × 10-15	10-60 s
Paired resistance training exercise 2	4-6 p.m.	3	65%-85%	2-3 × 10-15	10-60 s

Note: Paired exercises can include multijoint or single-joint exercises and traditional resistance training exercises or plyometric drills at low, moderate, or high intensity.

Conclusion

Concurrent training is the use of multiple modes of exercises in a training program over time to achieve multiple goals that typically include increasing cardiovascular fitness along with muscle hypertrophy, strength, and power. However, both historical and contemporary data continue to expose the reality that cardiovascular and resistance modes of training compete with one another at a molecular level. There is a preferential tendency to cancel out muscle hypertrophy, strength, and power improvements to salvage cardiovascular fitness.

Although concurrent training does not look promising for sports and athletics and elite fitness, there are some solutions, and those lie in strategic programming using the latest research and programming strategies to avoid muscle confusion and interference. The decision to include concurrent training in any program depends on programming goals, individual preferences, and the commitment to muscle hypertrophy, strength, and power goals over cardiovascular goals.

10 | Using Muscle Clocks to Improve Flexibility

Muscle pliability is a timing cue that muscle clocks look for and a primary stimulus for both muscle strength and power outcomes. However, because muscles need a certain degree of tension to produce force, it is tough to include flexibility training in a concurrent resistance and flexibility training program without diminishing muscle strength and power performance. This chapter focuses on how to design concurrent resistance and flexibility training programs that emphasize muscle strength and power development but also include flexibility exercises to improve muscle pliability and joint action.

Flexibility is defined as the ability of a muscle and connective tissues to relax and yield to stretch when lengthened. Because skeletal muscle fibers are arranged longitudinally, flexibility exercises are intended to lengthen a muscle from its origin to its insertion, stretching a muscle from one end to its opposite end.

Regular flexibility exercises both lengthen muscles and positively affect a joint's range of motion, or the maximal movement or greatest angle change allowed at a joint. Range of motion is determined by the pliability of muscles, tendons, and ligaments at any given joint and is influenced by factors such as age, sex (women are generally more flexible than men), fitness level, and type of activity. Muscle flexibility is important to resistance training results because a more pliable muscle can stretch more, allowing greater range of motion at the joint during an exercise. Full range of motion exercises are known to be of more use, especially in athletics, than short range of motion exercises that don't necessarily replicate functional and athletic movements.

Flexibility and Muscle Performance

Muscle pliability and joint range of motion are critical to fitness and athletic performance. When a muscle stretches, the muscle and its connective tissues and supporting tendons and ligaments are subjected to forces that affect pliability and joint range of motion, both of which are critical to muscle performance outcomes.

A stretched muscle produces greater force and thus greater strength and speed than a short muscle. Therefore, muscle performance is directly related to muscle length and flexibility.

In regard to muscle clocks, the pliability of tissues is also a critical timing cue. Muscle pliability provides muscle clocks valuable information about the time of day and mode of training, either resistance or flexibility, that provide anticipation cues to muscles about what type of training to expect and when, as well as activity–rest cycles.

Types of Stretching

In its broadest categorization, there are two types of stretching: self-stretching and partner-assisted stretching. Each type of stretching, although different in how it is applied, provides timing cues to muscle clocks about local tissue pliability.

Self-Stretching

There are three types of self-stretching: static (no movement), dynamic (movement), and ballistic (bouncing). As in physics, in stretching, the terms *static* and *dynamic* are used to describe whether an object is still (static) or on the move (dynamic). Think of a static system as a system that does not change. When athletes do static stretching, they put the muscle in a stretched position and hold it there. In other words, during static stretching a muscle stays in one place without movement.

In a dynamic system, however, athletes change positions in a controlled way. During all movement, the human body is a dynamic system; whether walking, lifting an external weight, or performing dynamic stretching, the body is active. A dynamic system is subject to changing positions and does so frequently. Dynamic stretching is often used before sports and exercise as a rhythmic or light warmup. Examples of dynamic stretching include knee to chest exercises and common forms of exercise such as tai chi and vinyasa flow yoga. Conventional wisdom advises dynamic stretching before exercise because the muscles and connective tissues are less pliable and at greater risk for injury.

One final mode of stretching that must be mentioned is ballistic. Ballistic stretching, like ballistic movement, is characterized by bouncing, jumping, or jerking. Although it is not uncommon to see athletes bounce through stretches as they attempt to work into a stretch, this type of stretching is advised against because muscles and connective tissues can easily be injured.

Partner-Assisted Stretching and Proprioceptive Neuromuscular Facilitation

Partner-assisted stretching is common in athletics and sports. Partner-assisted stretching differs from self-stretching in that the partner uses his or her body to move the athlete's body. Partner-assisted stretching can produce more stretch than self-stretching because the partner can apply more force using his or her body weight and gravity than an athlete can pulling on his or her own body. However, for this reason, partner-assisted stretching must be done with caution. When done correctly, partner-assisted stretching is more effective than self-stretching due to the partner's unique angle of approach. In partner-assisted stretching, the partner applies a push force (and, in some instances, a pull force) to the athlete to change the joint position, lengthen the muscles, produce stretching, and improve tissue pliability. However, to minimize the risks during partner-assisted stretching, the partner must be responsible for using body weight strategically and carefully as well as monitoring the athlete's stretching mechanics.

It is worth mentioning that there are other assisted stretching techniques that do not require a partner. These stretching methods incorporate an aid during static stretching, such as a calf muscle stretch done at the edge of a step or with the use of stretching strap or band.

Proprioceptive neuromuscular facilitation (PNF) is a method of partner-assisted stretching and is the most widely recognized stretching methodology. PNF stretching follows a five-step procedure.

1. Stretch the target muscle.
2. Contract the target muscle isometrically (without joint movement) for 5 to 6 s against resistance (usually a personal trainer, coach, or immovable object acts as the resistance). The intent is to inhibit movement of the contracting muscle or muscles. (*Note:* Never apply too much force or push too hard. Remember that the muscle spindle reflex will kick in and the muscle will recoil. Worse, severe muscle and/or joint injury can occur.)
3. Stretch the muscle again for 20 to 30 s.
4. Allow 30 s of recovery after the stretch.
5. Repeat 2 to 4 times.

To visualize PNF stretching, consider a cable system and the popular concept of resistance training agonist–antagonist muscle groups or functionally opposite muscles such as triceps and biceps muscles. For both stretching and resistance training, the principle of agonist–antagonist muscles is the same. For example, during resistance training when the biceps muscle contracts, the triceps muscle relaxes and vice versa. Another example is when the hip flexors lengthen, the lower back muscles shorten and vice versa.

It is essential to remember that the body uses muscles in an opposing manner. The key concept here is that when stretching one muscle, the functional opposite is also involved and must be considered as well. A best practice is to stretch the focus muscle and then its functional opposite. This complementary action allows for greater contraction of the targeted muscles and relies on two key physical structures: the Golgi tendon organs and the muscle spindles.

Golgi Tendon Organ

To work correctly, PNF stretching relies on the action of the Golgi tendon organ (GTO). The GTO is a small receptor located in the tendon that detects extreme ranges of motion. It is a built-in defense mechanism that prevents the muscle from being overstretched or the joints from overextending. Once in a stretched position, the muscle contraction stimulates the GTOs and that relaxes the muscle. The second thing that happens is that the muscle on the opposite side of the body or limb from the stretched muscle (the antagonist muscle) relaxes and allows more motion of the targeted muscle or muscles. Further analysis shows that when the GTO is activated during stretching, it sends a signal to the brain via the afferent (sensory) nerve, which causes a series of events in the brain, ultimately sending a command via the efferent (motor) nerve back to the same muscle to relax. The GTO essentially interrupts its own muscle's contraction, allowing stretch. Termed *autogenic inhibition,* this process allows the target muscle to stretch a little more and ultimately improves local tissue pliability.

Muscle Spindles

The other thing that happens during PNF stretching is reciprocal inhibition (RI). RI is controlled by the muscle spindles, which are tiny receptors that lie parallel to the muscle fibers and detect muscle length or stretching. When activated, the target muscle's spindles send a signal to the brain via afferent nerves, and the brain sends back a signal via motor nerves, causing the stretch reflex. The stretch reflex tells the opposing muscle to relax. When the opposing muscle relaxes, it allows more stretch of the target muscle. If the stretch is too much, the brain sends a signal to the muscle to contract and recoil in defense. Therefore, since tendons and ligaments have less pliability than muscle and the muscle itself has a defense to being overlengthened, stretching should be done with caution and focused intent.

Muscle spindles activate the stretch reflex used during the eccentric phase of training, particularly plyometric exercises, to increase muscle force output.

This process is an excellent example of how proprioceptive cues about muscle length are delivered to muscle clocks to help muscles determine when to anticipate training and what type of training to anticipate.

Muscle Pliability Is a Timing Cue

Muscle pliability changes as a function of each 24 h period and is a signaling cue to help muscle clocks determine the time of day and when to anticipate work versus rest. Tissue pliability is an indication of the natural elasticity of muscle, and it varies significantly from the time an athlete wakes to bedtime. In accordance with body temperature changes throughout the day, muscle tissue is least pliable first thing in the morning. As the day goes on, the natural elasticity of muscle increases, peaking between 4 and 6 p.m., indicating that muscles will be most flexible and able to lengthen the most efficiently during that time of day. Therefore muscle strength and power performance are best in the late afternoon to early evening. Local tissue pliability changes as a function of time of day are important because they show that muscles have a way to monitor their own natural cycles and set their own rhythms independent of the master clock.

The time of day a muscle is most pliable is an important time cue for muscle clocks and a factor in muscle performance because muscles generate their greatest force just beyond resting length or at about a joint angle of 110°. A slightly stretched muscle generates the most strength and power; therefore, any cues about muscle pliability delivered to muscle clocks will enhance muscle performance.

Time of Day

By now is it clear that all internal biological clocks, including muscle clocks, are on 24 h daily cycles. It is also apparent that all clocks use both external and internal cues to determine the time of day and coordinate tissue-specific actions to the time of day and the anticipated activity of local tissues. In the case of muscle clocks, the time of day of scheduled exercise is a critical entrainment cue. In relation to flexibility training, muscle pliability is a cue that helps muscle clocks recognize the time of day and make anticipatory adjustments ahead of training. Regularly scheduled exercise at a set time of day over the course of weeks and months helps muscle clocks set an internal 24 h rhythm and coordinate skeletal muscle tissue to anticipate resistance training sessions.

Muscles are most pliable when they are warm. Flexibility training, especially static stretching and any partner stretching, should be done after exercise or, at a minimum, after a light to moderate intensity warmup. Because body temperature peaks at 4 to 6 p.m., this means muscles are most ready to stretch around that time. This is also when muscles are their strongest, which helps

PNF stretching and explains why many athletes resistance train between 4 and 6 p.m. Although this time period isn't feasible for every athlete, it is important to understand the concept. An athlete who has been moving all day will have more pliable muscles than one who has just woken up.

Light–Dark Phase

Light is the most recognized time cue for setting and resetting biological clocks and rhythms. It is the most important time cue or circadian hook to the master clock. The master clock receives direct light input and sends signals directly to the peripheral clocks about day–night changes based on light cues alone.

Although light is the most studied cue and most widely recognized method to entrain biological clocks, scientists now know that biological clocks respond to a variety of time cues, setting and resetting their 24 h cycles in response to many different consistently delivered cues. In peripheral clocks, including muscle clocks, light along with multiple cues (such as muscle pliability changes over the course of the day) help muscle clocks recognize the time of day and anticipate upcoming flexibility training sessions.

Activity–Rest Pattern

Activity–rest patterns are partially determined by light–dark phases of a 24 h cycle. Humans tend to be more active during the day as a direct reflection of the circadian rhythm aligning itself to light–dark patterns established by the sun.

However, as discussed in chapter 1, activity–rest patterns may vary from person to person based on individual chronotype. A person's chronotype describes whether someone is a morning, midday, or night person. In addition to chronotype, social factors also influence activity–rest patterns, such as exercise training and programming schedules. It has been documented that muscle clocks shift based on the behavior of local muscle tissue (8). Scheduled flexibility training and time-of-day shifts in muscle pliability help reset muscle clocks according to an exercise training and programming schedule.

Regardless of chronotype, the master clock is aware of light–dark phases and works daily to keep the body on a 24 h schedule. For the most part, activity–rest patterns for the majority of people are coordinated to light–dark cycles by all internal clocks, including muscle clocks. Most people wake up naturally in the morning in alignment with the onset of daylight. At this time, tissues are least pliable. As the day goes on, body temperature rises, and with it, the muscle becomes more pliable and ready for exercise training and programming, such as flexibility training and eccentric training methods.

Muscle Length

The relationship between time of day, body temperature, muscle length, and pliability has been covered in detail. However, it is worth mentioning again that muscle pliability changes throughout the day and is a signaling cue to help muscle clocks determine the time of day and when to anticipate work or recovery. Time of day that a muscle is most pliable is an important cue for muscle clocks and a factor in muscle performance because muscles generate their greatest force just beyond resting length. A slightly stretched muscle generates the most strength and power.

Strength and Power Stimulus

Muscle stretch is a strength and power development stimulus. For example, plyometric exercises are explosive exercises that include jumping or quick movements, such as a barbell thrust during a machine lying chest press or a jump added to a squat or lunge, that focus on the eccentric action using the stretch reflex in muscles to produce power. Plyometric exercises are timing cues because they rely on muscles producing force during eccentric or lengthening action similar to muscle stretch. When a muscle stretches, it stimulates the onset of the mechanisms associated with muscle hypertrophy, strength, and power outcomes. Muscle length is also associated with strength performance because a muscle generates its greatest force at a joint angle around 110°. Therefore, pliability and the ability of a muscle to lengthen as trained by flexibility exercises help muscles click on the associated actions of muscle hypertrophy and strength and produce the optimal working lengths for the best performance outcomes. A final note on the value of a muscle lengthening to performance is that eccentric actions cause more human-growth-hormone (HGH) release than concentric actions (4).

Recovery Aid

The distinction between rest and recovery is critical. Rest is what an athlete does after working out and is a piece of the scheduling puzzle. Recovery, on the other hand, occurs both during sessions and after.

Recovery is active. During exercise, active recovery is something like walking or dynamic stretching between sets. Moving between sets readies the muscles, connective tissues, nervous system, and other supporting systems such as the heart for the next set. It is very active and an integral part of training. After training, recovery is even more vital. During recovery, the actual rebuilding of muscle occurs. During recovery, muscles engage in building and getting stronger. During training, intense exercise breaks down or catabolizes muscles, but, during postsession, recovery muscles rebuild or anabolize. In both cases, a lot is going on during recovery, and it is not passive.

On the other hand, rest is a vital part of the exercise training and programming schedule equation. Remember that muscle clocks and muscles learn to anticipate rest–activity periods. Over time, they reset to turn on the physiological mechanisms associated with muscle hypertrophy, strength, and power performance ahead of training.

Flexibility Programming

Current thought is that static stretching has an adverse effect on muscle performance. In a review of studies on the effects of static stretching on performance, the results showed that static stretching reduced maximal muscle strength, power, and speed (6). However, the effects of static stretching on performance depended on duration, or time in each stretch. Short durations of acute static stretches, defined as anything shorter than 30 s, did not result in a meaningful reduction in muscular performance. Stretches that were 30 to 45 s in duration reduced strength but not power. Finally, static stretches that were longer than 60 s reduced maximal performance on strength, power, and speed-dependent skills. The takeaway message is clear: The longer a static stretch is held before competition, the more likely it is to negatively affect all aspects of muscle performance (6).

Contrary to that review (6), Avloniti and colleagues (3) showed that static stretching can actually improve speed performance when each stretch is held for less than 30 s, while no negative or positive effects of static stretching were found for speed or agility at longer stretch times. Again, the takeaway message is apparent: The time in stretch appears to be the critical factor that will continue to be debated and studied.

The Avloniti study showed that short-duration (<30 s) static stretching before activity improved speed and agility performance, but only for moderately conditioned athletes (3). The bottom line is that time and conditioning level determine the effect static stretching has on muscle performance. Static stretching as a warmup should be implemented on a case-by-case basis. If used, each static stretch should be held for less than 30 s to avoid performance decrements.

Studies continue to indicate that dynamic stretching can be an effective way to improve muscle performance. One study showed that dynamic warmups, including dynamic stretching, increased quadriceps strength, a key factor in speed, before the activity (1).

The decision to use static or dynamic stretching before training, competition, and performance is tricky. A comprehensive review of studies on stretching and performance indicated a specific recommendation for dynamic stretching before activity, while PNF and static stretching are recommended after activity (5). The current recommendation is that if either PNF or static stretching is used before competition or training, provide at least 5 min of rest and include dynamic stretching. The intention is to allow muscles to recover contractility properties lost during static stretching before the event.

Static stretching in which each stretch is held for longer than 30 s appears to be best suited for after training and competition. Dynamic warmups, including dynamic stretching, are best suited for before competition and activity. As noted, if static stretching is used at all before competition or activity, keep the duration of each stretch shorter than 30 s and follow up with at least 5 min of dynamic warmup or stretching.

Stretching Mode

As discussed earlier, there are different types of stretching that will result in different muscle performance outcomes. They also provide muscle clocks with different cues about the condition of muscles, tendons, and ligaments.

Static

In static stretching, a stretch is obtained and held in one position. Just like a static system, a static stretch doesn't change or move. It stays in one place. When athletes do static stretching, they put the muscle in a stretched position and hold it there, resulting in a temporary change in muscle length that affects the contractile properties of the muscle. Static stretching as recommended as a postactivity exercise provides muscle clocks with timing cues about the time of day of training.

Dynamic

A dynamic system, as opposed to a static system, changes positions in a controlled way. During movement, whether walking or dynamic stretching, the human body is a dynamic system. A dynamic system is subject to changing positions and does so frequently. Dynamic stretching is often used before sports and exercise in the form of a rhythmic or light warmup. Dynamic stretching provides muscle clocks with additional information about the time of day of exercise and mode of exercise. Dynamic stretching, because it is recommended before exercise, can serve as an important source of information about the type of training and time of day of training for muscle clocks.

Timing of Stretching Relative to Training or Competition

Conventional wisdom advises against static stretching before exercise because the muscles and connective tissues are less pliable and at greater risk for injury. To the contrary, Avloniti and coworkers (2) showed that static stretching can actually improve speed performance when each stretch is held for less than 30 s, and no negative or positive effects of static stretching were found for speed or agility at longer stretch time. However, the suggested programming guide is to provide at least 5 min between static stretching and performance.

Whereas the debate continues over the value of static stretching to muscle performance, dynamic stretching can be an effective way to improve muscle performance. A study (1) showed that dynamic warm-ups, including dynamic stretching, increased quadriceps strength, a key factor in speed prior to muscle performance.

Duration

Static stretching in which each stretch is held for longer than 30 s appears to be best suited for after training and competition. This recommendation includes PNF stretching. Dynamic warmups, including dynamic stretching, are best used before competition and training. Again, if static stretching is used at all before competition or activity, keep the duration of each stretch shorter than 30 s and follow up with at least 5 min of a dynamic warmup or stretching.

Volume

Volume is the amount of exercise done during a training session and can be expressed as the amount of time spent jogging or the distance of a run, for example. With stretching, volume is reflected as the number of times a stretch is performed and the total time in the stretched position. Current recommendations include stretching 5 to 10 min each day for all major muscle groups combined (6). However, recommendations vary according to fitness level, goals, and sport-specific training demands.

Frequency

Training frequency describes how often exercise is done. Frequency most commonly is reflected as the number of days per week training is performed, but it can also be the number of sessions within days when more than one training session is done in a 24 h period. Flexibility training normally is done before and after each training session to some degree in any combination of static and dynamic and self-stretching or partner-assisted stretching. The frequency of stretching makes it a particularly useful exercise training and programming tool to use to reset muscle clocks. Because muscle clocks are closely monitoring the frequency and timing of training sessions within each 24 h period to anticipate and set a regular schedule, providing a regularly scheduled cue such as a muscle stretch that muscles recognize as a strength stimulus can help reset the muscle clocks and afford them the luxury of anticipation.

There are numerous opinions on the frequency of different types of stretching and when they should be done to improve flexibility. Few studies have been done on the topic of the frequency of stretching for best results. One study showed that stretching must be done 5 days per week for at least 6 weeks before improvements in flexibility are seen (7). This frequency might be unrealistic in some training settings, so the current recommendation is that sport and athletic and fitness trainers incorporate stretching into each session when possible and encourage athletes and clients to stretch alone as well.

Table 10.1 provides a sample program of static stretching and flexibility training within a concurrent training program for muscle strength and power.

TABLE 10.1 Sample Program for Flexibility Training within a Concurrent Training Program for Muscle Strength and Power

Day	Type of stretching	Duration of stretch before event or training	Rest between stretching and training or event	Duration of stretch after event or training
Sunday	Static	<30 s	5 min	≥30 s
Monday	Static	<30 s	5 min	≥30 s
Tuesday	Static	<30 s	5 min	≥30 s
Wednesday	Static	<30 s	5 min	≥30 s
Thursday	Static	<30 s	5 min	≥30 s
Friday	Static	<30 s	5 min	≥30 s
Saturday	Static	<30 s	5 min	≥30 s

Note: The same program strategy can be used for training programs that include two workouts per day.

Programming Summary Statements

The following flexibility training programming summary statements are intended for use when optimal muscle performance, particularly muscle strength and power, during training and competition is the intended goal instead of general flexibility.

- Before training or events, keep static stretches to less than 30 s.
- If static stretching is used before training or events, provide at least 5 min of dynamic activity between stretching and performance.
- As a general rule, use dynamic stretching before training and events.
- Do static stretches in which each stretch is held longer than 30 s after a sport event or training.

Conclusion

During flexibility training, both the muscle and its connective tissues are subjected to forces. This means that the muscle body, its tendons, and the supporting ligaments are all affected by stretching and subject to the possible interference with muscle contractility caused by stretching. However, muscle stretch is a powerful strength stimulus, and local tissue pliability in muscles is an important timing cue delivered to muscle clocks about the time of day and when to anticipate exercise training.

REFERENCES

Chapter 1

1. Andrews JL, Zhang X, McCarthy JJ, et al. CLOCK and BMAL1 regulate MyoD and are necessary for maintenance of skeletal muscle phenotype and function. *Proc Natl Acad Sci U S A*. 2010;107:19090-19095.

2. Barger LK, Wright KP, Hughes RJ, Czeisler CA. Daily exercise facilitates phase delays of circadian melatonin rhythm in very dim light. *Am J Physiol Regul Integr Comp Physiol*. 2004;286(6):R1077-R1084.

3. Bunger MK, Walisser JA, Sullivan R, et al. Progressive arthropathy in mice with a targeted disruption of the Mop3/Bmal-1 locus. *Genesis*. 2005;41:122-132.

4. Chatterjee S, Yin H, Nam D, Li Y, Ma K. Brain and muscle Arnt-like 1 promotes skeletal muscle regeneration through satellite cell expansion. *Exp Cell Res*. 2015;331:200-210.

5. Chauhan R, Chen KF, Kent BA, Crowther DC. Central and peripheral circadian clocks and their role in Alzheimer's disease. *Dis Model Mech*. 2017;10(10):1187-1199.

6. Dibner C, Schibler U, Albrecht U. The mammalian circadian timing system: organization and coordination of central and peripheral clocks. *Ann Rev Physiol*. 2010;72:517-549.

7. Dudek M, Meng QJ. Running on time: the role of circadian clocks in the musculoskeletal system. *Biochem J. 2014*;463(1):1-8.

8. Dyar KA, Ciciliot S, Tagliazucchi GM, et al. The calcineurin-NFAT pathway controls activity-dependent circadian gene expression in slow skeletal muscle. *Mol Metab*. 2015;4:823-833.

9. Edgar D, Dement W. Regularly scheduled voluntary exercise synchronizes the mouse circadian clock. *Am J Physiol*. 1991;261:R928-R33.

10. Facer-Childs E, Brandstaetter R. The impact of circadian phenotype and time since awakening on diurnal performance in athletes. *Curr Biol*. 2015;25:518-522.

11. Kondratov RV, Kondratova AA, Gorbacheva VY, Vykhovanets OV, Antoch MP. Early aging and age-related pathologies in mice deficient in BMAL1, the core component of the circadian clock. *Genes Dev*. 2006;20:1868-1873.

12. Marcheva B, Moynihan Ramsey K, Buhr ED. Disruption of the clock components CLOCK and BMAL1 leads to hypoinsulinemia and diabetes. *Nature*. 2010;466:627-631.

13. McCarthy JJ, Andrews JL, McDearmon EL, et al. Identification of the circadian transcriptome in adult mouse skeletal muscle. *Physiol Genomics*. 2007;31:86-95.

14. Miller BH, McDearmon EL, Panda S, et al. Circadian and CLOCK-controlled regulation of the mouse transcriptome and cell proliferation. *Proc Natl Acad Sci U S A*. 2007;104:3342-3347.

15. Murphy BA, Wagner AL, McGlynn OF, Kharazyan F, Browne JA, Elliott JA. Exercise influences circadian gene expression in equine skeletal muscle. *Vet*. 2014; 201: 39-45.

16. Pedersen L, Hojman P. Muscle-to-organ cross talk mediated by myokines. *Adipocyte*. 2012;1:164-167.

17. Reeds PJ, Palmer RM, Hay SM, McMillan DN. Protein synthesis in skeletal muscle measured at different times during a 24 hour period. *Biosci Rep.* 1986;6:209-213.

18. Roenneberg T, Merrow M. Circadian clocks: the fall and rise of physiology. *Nat Rev Mol Cell Biol.* 2005;6:965-971.

19. Samsa WE, Vasanji A, Midura RJ, Kondratov RV. Deficiency of circadian clock protein BMAL1 in mice results in a low bone mass phenotype. *Bone.* 2016;84:194-203.

20. Schroder EA, Esser KA. Circadian rhythms, skeletal muscle molecular clocks and exercise. *Exerc Sport Sci Rev.* 2013;41(4):224-229.

21. Schroeder AM, Truong D, Loh DH, Jordan MC, Roos KP, Colwell CS. Voluntary scheduled exercise alters diurnal rhythms of behaviour, physiology and gene expression in wild-type and vasoactive intestinal peptide-deficient mice. *J Physiol.* 2012;590(23):6213-6226.

22. Sedliak M, Finni T, Cheng S, Lind M, Häkkinen K. Effect of time-of-day-specific strength training on muscular hypertrophy in men. *J Strength Cond Res.* 2009;23:2451-2457.

23. Souissi H, Chtourou H, Chaouachi A, et al. The effect of training at a specific time-of-day on the diurnal variations of short-term exercise performances in 10- to 11-year-old boys. *Pediatr Exerc Sci.* 2012;24:84-99.

24. Stephan FK, Zucker I. Circadian rhythms in drinking behavior and locomotor activity of rats are eliminated by hypothalamic lesions. *Proc Natl Acad Sci U S A.* 1972;69:1583-1586.

25. Takahashi JS, Hong HK, Ko CH, McDearmon EL. The genetics of mammalian circadian order and disorder: implications for physiology and disease. *Nat Rev Genet.* 2008;9:764-775.

26. Wolff G, Esser KA. Scheduled exercise phase shifts the circadian clock in skeletal muscle. *Med Sci Sports Exerc.* 2012;44(9):1663-1670.

27. Zambon A, McDearmon E, Salomonis N, et al. (2003). Time and exercise-dependent gene regulation in human skeletal muscle. *Genome Biol.* 2003;4(10):R61.

28. Zhang X, Dube TJ, Esser K A. Working around the clock: circadian rhythms and skeletal muscle. *J Appl Physiol.* 2009;107:1647-1654.

29. Zylka MJ, Shearman LP, Weaver DR, Reppert SM. Three period homologs in mammals: differential light responses in the suprachiasmatic circadian clock and oscillating transcripts outside of brain. *Neuron.* 2009;20:1103-1110.

Chapter 2

1. Beck TW, DeFreitas JM, Stock MS. The effects of a resistance training program on average motor unit firing rates. *Clin Kinesiol.* 2011;65(1):1-8.

2. Carter J, Greenwood M. Complex training reexamined: review and recommendations to improve strength and power. *Strength Cond J.* 2014;36(2):11-19.

3. de Souza EO, Tricoli V, Franchini E, Paulo AC, Regazzini M, Ugrinowitsch C. Acute effect of two aerobic exercise modes on maximum strength and strength endurance. *J Strength Cond Res.* 2007;21:1286-1290.

4. Docherty D, Sporer B. A proposed model for examining the interference phenomenon between concurrent aerobic and strength training. *Sports Med.* 2000;30(6):385-394.

5. Doma K, Deakin G. The cumulative effects of strength and endurance training sessions on muscle force generation capacity over four days. *J Aust Strength Cond.* 2013;21(suppl 1):34-38.

6. Fyfe JJ, Bartlett JD, Hanson ED, Stepto NK, Bishop DJ. Endurance training intensity does not mediate interference to maximal lower-body strength gain during short-term concurrent training. *Front Physiol*. 2016;7:1-16.

7. Fyfe JJ, Bishop DJ, Stepto NK. Interference between concurrent resistance and endurance exercise: molecular bases and the role of individual training variables. *Sports Med*. 2014;44(6):743-762.

8. Gomes KG, Franco CM, Nunes PRP, Orsatti FL. High-frequency resistance training is not more effective than low-frequency resistance training in increasing muscle mass and strength in well-trained men. *J Strength Cond Res*. 2018;1:10.

9. Gupta L, Morgan K, Gilchrist S. Does elite sport degrade sleep quality? A systematic review. *Sports Med*. 2017;47(7):1317-1333.

10. Hakkinen K, Alen M, Kraemer WJ, et al. Neuromuscular adaptations during concurrent strength and endurance training versus strength training. *Eur J Appl Physiol*. 2003;89:42-52.

11. Hickson RC. Interference of strength development by simultaneously training for strength and endurance. *Eur J Appl Physiol Occup Physiol*. 1980;45:255-263.

12. Jones TW, Howatson G, Russell M, French DN. Effects of strength and endurance exercise order on endocrine responses to concurrent training. *Eur J Sport Sci*. 2017;17(3):326-334.

13. Kikuchi N, Yoshida S, Okuyama M, Nakazato K. The effect of high-intensity interval cycling sprints subsequent to arm-curl exercise on upper-body muscle strength and hypertrophy. *J Strength Cond Res*. 2016;30(8):2318-2323.

14. Losnegard T, Mikkelsen K, Ronnestad BR, Hallen J, Rud B, Raastad T. The effect of heavy strength training on muscle mass and physical performance in elite cross country skiers. *Scand J Med Sci Sports*. 2011;21(3):389-401.

15. Mikkola J, Rusko H, Izquierdo M, Gorostiaga EM, Hakkinen K. Neuromuscular and cardiovascular adaptations during concurrent strength and endurance training in untrained men. *Int J Sports Med*. 2012;33:702-710.

16. Mirghani SJ, Alinejad HA, Azarbayjani MA, Mazidi A. Influence of strength, endurance and concurrent training on the lipid profile and blood testosterone and cortisol response in young male wrestlers. *Baltic J Health Phys Act*. 2014;6(3):7-16.

17. Murach KA, Bagley JA. Skeletal muscle hypertrophy with concurrent exercise training: contrary evidence for an interference effect. *Sports Med*. 2016;46(8):1029-1039.

18. Petré H, Löfving P, Psilander N. The effect of two different concurrent training programs on strength and power gains in highly-trained individuals. *J Sports Sci Med*. 2018;17:167-173.

19. Robineau J, Babault N, Piscione J, Lacome M, Bigard AX. The specific training effects of concurrent aerobic and strength exercises depends upon recovery duration. *J Strength Cond Res*. 2016;30(3):672-683.

20. Wilson JM, Marin PJ, Rhea MR, Wilson SM, Loenneke JP, Anderson JC. Concurrent training: a meta-analysis examining interference of aerobic and resistance exercises. *J Strength Cond Res*. 2012;26(8):2293-2307.

Chapter 3

1. Andrada RT, Maynar M, Muñoz D, Maríno JIM. Variations in urine excretion of steroid hormones after an acute session and after a 4-week programme of strength training *Eur J Appl Physiol*. 2007;99:65.

2. Calixto R, Verlengia, R, Crisp A, et al. Acute effects of movement velocity on blood lactate and growth hormone responses after eccentric bench press exercise in resistance-trained men. *Biol Sport*. 2015;31(4):289-294.

3. Crewther B, Keogh J, Cronin J, Cook C. Possible stimuli for strength and power adaptation: acute hormonal responses. *Sports Med*. 2006;36(3):215-238.

4. Dibner C, Schibler U, Albrecht U. The mammalian circadian timing system: organization and coordination of central and peripheral clocks. *Ann Rev Physiol*. 2007;72:517-549.

5. Dudek M, Meng QJ. Running on time: the role of circadian clocks in the musculoskeletal system. *Biochem J*. 2014;463(1):1-8.

6. Duffy JF, Wright KP. Entrainment of the human circadian system by light. *J Biol Rhythms*. 2005;20:326-338.

7. Godfrey RJ, Madgwick Z, Whyte G. The exercise-induced growth hormone response in athletes. *Sports Med*. 2003;33:599-613.

8. Jakob LV, Kraemer WJ, Ratamess NA, Anderson JM, Volek JS, Maresh CM. Testosterone physiology in resistance exercise and training: the up-stream regulatory elements. *Sports Med*. 2010;40(12):1037-1053.

9. Jones TW, Howatson G, Russell M, French DN. Effects of strength and endurance exercise order on endocrine responses to concurrent training. *Eur J Sports Sci*. 2017;17(3):326-334.

10. Mayeuf-Louchart A, Staels B, Duez H. Skeletal muscle functions around the clock. *Diabetes Obes Metab*. 2015;17(suppl 1):39-46.

11. Murach KA, Bagley JA. Skeletal muscle hypertrophy with concurrent exercise training: contrary evidence for an interference effect. *Sports Med*. 2016;46(8):1029–1039.

12. Oliver JM, Jagim AR, Sanchez AC, et al. Greater gains in strength and power with intra-set rest intervals in hypertrophic training. *J Strength Cond Res*. 2013;27(11):3116-3131.

13. Roenneberg T., Merrow M. Circadian clocks: the fall and rise of physiology. *Nat Rev Mol Cell Biol*. 2005;6:965-971.

14. Sasaki H, Hattori Y, Ikeda Y, et al. Forced rather than voluntary exercise entrains peripheral clocks via a corticosterone/noradrenaline increase in PER2::LUC mice. *Sci Rep*. 2016;6:27607.

15. Sasaki H, Ohtsu T, Ikeda Y, Tsubosaka M, Shibata S. Combination of meal and exercise timing with a high-fat diet influences energy expenditure and obesity in mice. *Chronobiol Int*. 2014;31:959-975.

16. Skeldon AC, Phillips AJ, Dijk DJ. The effects of self-selected light-dark cycles and social constraints on human sleep and circadian timing: a modeling approach. *Sci Rep*. 2017;7:45158.

17. Smilios I, Theophilos P, Karamouzis M, Parlavantzas A, Tokmakidis S. Hormonal responses after a strength endurance resistance exercise protocol in young and elderly males. *Int J Sports Med*. 2007;28:401-409.

18. Takahashi JS, Hong HK, Ko CH, McDearmon EL. The genetics of mammalian circadian order and disorder: implications for physiology and disease. *Nat Rev Genet.* 2008;9:764-775.

19. Wilson JM, Marin PJ, Rhea MR, Wilson SM, Loenneke JP, Anderson JC. Concurrent training: a meta-analysis examining interference of aerobic and resistance exercises. *J Strength Cond Res.* 2012;26(8):2293-2307.

Chapter 4

1. Carter J, Greenwood M. Complex training reexamined: review and recommendations to improve strength and power. *Strength Cond J.* 2014;36(2):11-19.

2. Slater L, Hart J. Muscle activation patterns during different squat techniques. *J Strength Cond Res.* 2016;31(1):667-676.

Chapter 5

1. Antle M, Silver R. Neural basis of timing and anticipatory behaviors. *Eur J Neurosci.* 2009;30:1643-1649.

2. Mayeuf-Louchart A, Staels B, and Duez H. Skeletal muscle functions around the clock. *Diabetes Obes Metab.* 2015;17(suppl 1):39-46.

3. Norrie ML. Effects of movement complexity on choice reaction and movement times. *Res Q.* 1974;45(2):154-161.

4. Oliver JM, Jagim AR, Sanchez AC, et al. Greater gains in strength and power with intra-set rest intervals in hypertrophic training. *J Strength Cond Res.* 2013;27(11):3116-3131.

5. Stöckel T, Wunsch K, Hughes CML. Age-related decline in anticipatory motor planning and its relation to cognitive and motor skill proficiency. *Front Aging Neurosci.* 2017;9:1-12.

6. Schroder EA, Esser KA. Circadian rhythms, skeletal muscle molecular clocks and exercise. *Exer Sport Sci Rev.* 2013;41(4):224-229.

7. Wright MJ, Bishop DT, Jackson RC, Abernethy B. Brain regions concerned with the identification of deceptive soccer moves by higher-skilled and lower-skilled players. *Front Hum Neurosci.* 2013;7:851.

Chapter 6

1. Beck TW, DeFreitas JM, Stock MS. The effects of a resistance training program on average motor unit firing rates. *Clin Kinesiol.* 2011;65(1):1-8.

2. Doma K, Deakin G. The cumulative effects of strength and endurance training sessions on muscle force generation capacity over four days. *J Aust Strength Cond.* 2013;21(suppl 1):34-38.

3. Fyfe JJ, Bishop DJ, Stepto NK. Interference between concurrent resistance and endurance exercise: molecular bases and the role of individual training variables. *Sports Med.* 2014;44(6):743-762.

4. Gonzalo-Skok Ó, Tous-Fajardo J, Suarez-Arrones LJ, Arjol-Serrano JL, Casajus JA, Mendez-villanueva A. Single-leg power output and between-limbs imbalances in team-sport players: unilateral versus bilateral combined resistance training. *Int J Sports Physiol Perform.* 2017;12(1):*106-114.*

5. Gupta L, Morgan K, Gilchrist S. Does elite sport degrade sleep quality? A systematic review. *Sports Med.* 2017;47(7):1317-1333.

6. Hammami M, Negra Y, Roy S, Mohamed Souhaiel C. The effect of standard strength vs. contrast strength training on the development of sprint, agility, repeated change of direction and jump in male junior soccer players. *J Strength Cond Res.* 2017;31:1.

7. Kreher JB. Diagnosis and prevention of overtraining syndrome: an opinion on education strategies. *J Sports Med.* 2016;7:115-122.

8. Radak Z, Chung HY, Koltai E, et al. Exercise, oxidative stress and hormesis. *Ageing Res Rev.* 2008;7(1):34-42.

9. Soares S, Ferreira-Junior JB, Pereira MC, et al. Dissociated time course of muscle damage recovery between single- and multi-joint exercises in highly resistance-trained men. *J Strength Cond Res.* 2015;29(9):2594-2599.

10. Stasinaki AE, Gloumis G, Spengos KM, et al. Muscle strength, power, and morphologic adaptations after 6 weeks of compound vs. complex training in healthy men. *J Strength Cond Res.* 2015;29(9):2559-2569.

Chapter 7

1. Amirthalingam T, Mavros Y, Wilson GC, Clarke JL, Mitchell L, Hackett DA. Effects of a modified german volume training program on muscular hypertrophy and strength. *J Strength Cond Res.* 2017;31(11):3109-3119.

2. Botton CE, Radaelli R, Wilhelm EN, Rech A, Brown LE, Pinto RS. Neuromuscular adaptations to unilateral vs. bilateral strength training in women. *J Strength Cond Res.* 2016;30(7):1924-1932.

3. Crewther B, Keogh J, Cronin J, Cook C. Possible stimuli for strength and power adaptation: acute hormonal responses. *Sports Med.* 2006;36(3):215-238.

4. Jenkins ND, Housh TJ, Buckner SL, et al. Neuromuscular adaptations after 2 and 4 weeks of 80% versus 30% 1 repetition maximum resistance training to failure. *J Strength Cond Res.* 2016;30(8):2174-2185.

5. Oliver JM, Jagim AR, Sanchez AC, et al. Greater gains in strength and power with intra-set rest intervals in hypertrophic training. *J Strength Cond Res.* 2013;27(11):3116-3131.

6. Ozaki H, Kubota A, Natsume T, et al. Effects of drop sets with resistance training on increases in muscle CSA, strength, and endurance: a pilot study. *J Sports Sci.* 2018;36(6):691-696.

7. Paoli A, Gentil P, Moro T, Marcolin G, Bianco A. Resistance training with single vs. multi-joint exercises at equal total load volume: effects on body composition, cardiorespiratory fitness, and muscle strength. *Front Physiol.* 2015;8:1105.

8. Radaelli R, Fleck SJ, Leite T, et al. Dose-response of 1, 3, and 5 sets of resistance exercise on strength, local muscular endurance, and hypertrophy. *J Strength Cond Res.* 2015;29(5):1349-1358.

9. Saeterbakken A, Andersen V, Brudeseth A, Lund H, Fimland MS. The effect of performing bi- and unilateral row exercises on core muscle activation. *Int J Sports Med.* 2015;36(11):900-905.

10. Smilios I, Theophilos P, Karamouzis M, Parlavantzas A, Tokmakidis S. Hormonal responses after a strength endurance resistance exercise protocol in young and elderly males. *Int J Sports Med.* 2007;28:401-409.

Chapter 8

1. Carter J, Greenwood M. Complex training reexamined: review and recommendations to improve strength and power. *Strength Cond J.* 2014;36(2):11-19.

2. Crewther B, Keogh J, Cronin J, Cook C. Possible stimuli for strength and power adaptation: acute hormonal responses. *Sports Med.* 2006;36(3):215-238.

3. Juarez D, Gonzalez-Rave JM, Navarro F. Effects of complex vs. noncomplex training programs on lower body maximum strength and power. *Isokinet Exerc Sci.* 2009;17:233-241.

4. Paoli A, Gentil P, Moro T, Marcolin G, Bianco A. Resistance training with single vs. multi-joint exercises at equal total load volume: effects on body composition, cardiorespiratory fitness, and muscle strength. *Front Physiol.* 2015;8:1105.

5. Potach DH, Chu DA. Plyometric training. In: Baechle TR, Earle RW, eds. *Essentials of Strength Training and Conditioning.* Champaign, IL: Human Kinetics; 2008:413-456.

6. Smilios I, Theophilos P, Karamouzis M, Parlavantzas A, Tokmakidis S. Hormonal responses after a strength endurance resistance exercise protocol in young and elderly males. *Int J Sports Med.* 2007;28:401-409.

7. Tufano JJ, Conlon JA, Nimphius S, et al. Maintenance of velocity and power with cluster sets during high-volume back squats. *Int J Sports Physiol Perform.* 2016;11(7):885-892.

Chapter 9

1. Beck TW, DeFreitas JM, Stock MS. The effects of a resistance training program on average motor unit firing rates. *Clin Kinesiol.* 2011;65(1):1-8.

2. Browne GJ, Proud CG. Regulation of peptide-chain elongation in mammalian cells. *Eur J Biochem.* 2002;269:5360-5368.

3. Chromiak J, Mulvaney D. The effects of combined strength and endurance training on strength development. *J Appl Sports Sci Res.* 1990;4:55-60.

4. Costill DL, Bowers R, Branam G, Sparks K. Muscle glycogen utilization during prolonged exercise on successive days. *J Appl Physiol.* 1971;31:834-838.

5. Creer A, Gallaoher P, Slivka D, Jemiolo B, Fink W, Trappe S. Influence of muscle glycogen availability on ERKI/2 and Akt signaling after resistance exercise in human skeletal muscle. *J Appl Physiol.* 2005;99:950-956.

6. Docherty D, Sporer B. A proposed model for examining the interference phenomenon between concurrent aerobic and strength training. *Sports Med.* 2000;30(6):385-394.

7. Doma K, Deakin G. The cumulative effects of strength and endurance training sessions on muscle force generation capacity over four days. *J Aust Strength Cond.* 2013;21(suppl 1):34-38.

8. Dudley GA, Djamil R. Incompatibility of endurance and strength-training modes of exercise. *J Appl Physiol.* 1985;59:1446-1451.

9. Eklund D, Pulverenti T, Bankers S, et al. Neuromuscular adaptations to different modes of combined strength and endurance training. *Int J Sports Med.* 2014;36:120-129.

10. Fyfe JJ, Bishop DJ, Stepto NK. Interference between concurrent resistance and endurance exercise: molecular bases and the role of individual training variables. *Sports Med.* 2014;44(6):743-762.

11. Hernandez JM, Fedele MJ, Farrell PA. Time course evaluation of protein synthesis and glucose uptake after acute resistance exercise in rats. *J Appl Physiol.* 2000;88(3):1142-1149.

12. Hickson RC Interference of strength development by simultaneously training for strength and endurance. *Eur J Appl Physiol Occup Physiol.* 1980;45:255-263.

13. Jones TW, Howatson G, Russell M, French DN. Effects of strength and endurance exercise order on endocrine responses to concurrent training. *Eur J Sports Sci.* 2017;17(3):326-334.

14. Kikuchi N, Yoshida S, Okuyama M, Nakazato K. The effect of high-intensity interval cycling sprints subsequent to arm-curl exercise on upper-body muscle strength and hypertrophy. *J Strength Cond Res.* 2016;30(8):2318-2323.

15. Kraemer WJ., Patton F, Gordon E, et al. Compatibility of high-intensity strength and endurance training on hormonal and skeletal muscle adaptations. *J Appl Physiol.* 1995;78:976-989.

16. Kuipers H, Keizer HA. Overtraining in elite athletes. Review and directions for the future. *Sports Med.* 1988;6:79-92.

17. Küüsmaa-Schildt M, Eklund D, Avela J, et al. Neuromuscular adaptations to combined strength and endurance training: order and time-of-day. *Int J Sports Med.* 2017;38:707-716.

18. Luginbuhl AJ, Dudley GA, Staron HS. Fiber type changes in rat skeletal muscle after intense interval training. *Histochemistry.* 1984;81:55-58.

19. Murach KA, Bagley JA. Skeletal muscle hypertrophy with concurrent exercise training: contrary evidence for an interference effect. *Sports Med.* 2016;46(8):1029-1039.

20. Nader GA, Esser KA. Intracellular signaling specificity in skeletal muscle in response to different modes of exercise. *J Appl Physiol.* 2001;90:1936-1942.

21. Rose AJ, Broholm C, Kiillerich K, et al. Exercise rapidly increases eukaryotic elongation factor 2 phosphorylation in skeletal muscle of men. *J Physiol.* 2005;569:223-228.

22. Schumann M, Pelttari P, Doma K, Karavirta L, Häkkinen K. Neuromuscular adaptations to same-session combined endurance and strength training in recreational endurance runners. *Int J Sports Med.* 2016;37(14):1136-1143.

23. Tesch PA, Colliander AB, Kaiser P. Muscle metabolism during intense, heavy-resistance exercise. *Eur J Appl Physiol Occup Physiol.* 1986;55:362-366.

24. Wilson JM, Marin PJ, Rhea MR, Wilson SM, Loenneke JP, Anderson JC. Concurrent training: a meta-analysis examining interference of aerobic and resistance exercises. *J Strength Cond Res* 2012;26(8):2293-2307.

25. Winder WW. Energy-sensing and signaling by AMP-activated protein kinase in skeletal muscle. *J Appl Physiol.* 2001;91:1017-1028.

26. Wojtaszewski JF, Macdonald C, Nielsen JN, et al. Regulation of 5\p\AMP-activated protein kinase activity and substrate utilization in exercising human skeletal muscle. *Am J Physiol Endocrinol Metab.* 2003;284:E813-E822.

27. Wolff G, Esser KA. Scheduled exercise phase shifts the circadian clock in skeletal muscle. *Med Sci Sports Exerc.* 2012;44(9):1663-1670.

Chapter 10

1. Aguilar AJ, DiStefano LJ, Brown CN, Herman DC, Guskiewicz KM, Padua DA. A dynamic warm-up model increases quadriceps strength and hamstring flexibility. *Eur J Sport Sci.* 2016;16(4):402-408.

2. Avloniti A, Chatzinikolaou A, Fatouros IG, et al. The acute effects of static stretching on speed and agility performance depend on stretch duration and conditioning level. *J Strength Cond Res.* 2016;30(10):2767-2773.

3. Avloniti A, Chatzinikolaou A, Fatouros IG, et al. The effects of static stretching on speed and agility: one or multiple repetition protocols? *J Strength Cond Res.* 2011;25(11):2991-2998.

4. Crewther B, Keogh J, Cronin J, Cook C. Possible stimuli for strength and power adaptation: acute hormonal responses. *Sports Med. 2006;*36(3):215-238.

5. Peck E, Chomko G, Gaz DV, Farrell AM. The effects of stretching on performance. *Curr Sports Med Rep.* 2014;13(3):179-183.

6. Shrier I, McHugh M. Does static stretching reduce maximal muscle performance? A review. *Clin J Sports Med.* 2012;22(5):450-451.

7. Wiley RW, Kyle BA, Moore SA, Chleboun GS. Effect of cessation and resumption of static hamstring muscle stretching on joint range of motion. *J Orthop Sports Phys Ther* 2001;31(3):138-144.

8. Wolff G, Esser KA. Scheduled exercise phase shifts the circadian clock in skeletal muscle. *Med Sci Sports Exerc.* 2012;44(9):1663-1670.

INDEX

Note: The italicized f and t following page numbers refer to figures and tables, respectively.

ABOUT THE AUTHOR

Amy Ashmore holds a PhD in kinesiology from the University of Texas at Austin and an MS in exercise science from Florida State University. She is the author of dozens of articles, blogs, and continuing education programs recognized by the National Strength and Conditioning Association (NSCA), Collegiate Strength and Conditioning Coaches Association (CSCCa), American Council on Exercise (ACE), and American College of Sports Medicine (ACSM). Amy was previously on the sports sciences faculty at Florida State University and is the former program director for sports sciences and sports management at American Military University. She is an author and continuing education provider located in Las Vegas, Nevada.